HBJ TREASURY OF LITERATU

Up One Hill and Down Another

SENIOR AUTHORS
ROGER C. FARR
DOROTHY S. STRICKLAND

AUTHORS
RICHARD F. ABRAHAMSON
ELLEN BOOTH CHURCH
BARBARA BOWEN COULTER
MARGARET A. GALLEGO
JUDITH L. IRVIN
KAREN KUTIPER
JUNKO YOKOTA LEWIS
DONNA M. OGLE
TIMOTHY SHANAHAN
PATRICIA SMITH

SENIOR CONSULTANTS
BERNICE E. CULLINAN
W. DORSEY HAMMOND
ASA G. HILLIARD III

CONSULTANTS
ALONZO A. CRIM
ROLANDO R. HINOJOSA-SMITH
LEE BENNETT HOPKINS
ROBERT J. STERNBERG

HARCOURT BRACE & COMPANY
Orlando   Atlanta   Austin   Boston   San Francisco   Chicago   Dallas   New York
Toronto   London

Printed in the United States of America

ISBN 0-15-300419-3

3 4 5 6 7 8 9 10   048   96   95   94   93

Acknowledgments continue on page 310, which constitutes an extension of this copyright page.

Acknowledgments

For permission to reprint copyrighted material, grateful acknowledgment is made to the following sources:

Atheneum Publishers, an imprint of Macmillan Publishing Company: "Reply to Someone Who Asked Why the Two of Us Are Such Good Friends" from *A Week in the Life of Best Friends* by Beatrice Schenk de Regniers. Text copyright © 1986 by Beatrice Schenk de Regniers.

Bantam Books, a division of Bantam Doubleday Dell Publishing Group, Inc.: "Junk Day on Juniper Street" from *Junk Day on Juniper Street* by Lilian Moore. Text copyright © 1969 by Lilian Moore.

Curtis Brown, Ltd.: "We're Racing, Racing down the Walk" from *Sugar and Spice: The ABC of Being a Girl* by Phyllis McGinley. Text copyright © 1959, 1960 by Phyllis McGinley.

Childrens Press, Inc.: Fiesta! by June Behrens. Text copyright © 1978 by Childrens Press®, Inc.

Clarion Books, a Houghton Mifflin Company imprint: Cover illustration by James Ransome from *Aunt Flossie's Hats (and Crab Cakes Later)* by Elizabeth Fitzgerald. Illustration copyright © 1991 by James Ransome.

Doubleday, a division of Bantam Doubleday Dell Publishing Group, Inc.: "Celebration" by Alonzo Lopez from *Whispering Wind* by Terry Allen. Text copyright © 1972 by the Institute of American Indian Arts. From *The Playtime Treasury* (Retitled: "Games of Chase . . . Catch . . . Tip . . . Tiggy . . . Tick . . . Touch . . . It . . . Tag . . .") by Pie Corbett. Text copyright © 1989 by Pie Corbett.

Farrar, Straus & Giroux, Inc.: "two friends" from *Spin a Soft Black Song* by Nikki Giovanni. Text copyright © 1971, 1985 by Nikki Giovanni.

Greenwillow Books, a division of William Morrow & Company, Inc.: Cover illustration from *Chester's Way* by Kevin Henkes. Copyright © 1988 by Kevin Henkes. Cover illustration by Victoria Chess from *Once Around the Block* by Kevin Henkes. Illustration copyright © 1987 by Victoria Chess. "The Lion and the Mouse" from *Once in a Wood* by Eve Rice. Copyright © 1979 by Eve Rice.

Harcourt Brace Jovanovich, Inc.: Little Penguin's Tale by Audrey Wood. Copyright © 1989 by Audrey Wood.

HarperCollins Publishers: Poinsettia and the Firefighters by Felicia Bond. Copyright © 1984 by Felicia Bond. Cover illustration by Susan Truesdell from *Donna O'Neeshuck Was Chased By Some Cows* by Bill Grossman. Illustration copyright © 1988 by Susan G. Truesdell. Cover illustration by Megan Lloyd from *Surprises* by Lee Bennett Hopkins. Illustration copyright © 1984 by Megan Lloyd. Cover illustration by Joan Sandin from *Hill of Fire* by Thomas P. Lewis. Illustration copyright © 1971 by Joan Sandin. Cover illustration from *Frog and Toad Are Friends* by Arnold Lobel. Copyright © 1970 by Arnold Lobel. *I Have a Sister—My Sister Is Deaf* by Jeanne Whitehouse Peterson. Text copyright © 1977 by Jeanne Whitehouse Peterson.

Holiday House: Cover illustration by Robert Casilla from *A Picture Book of Martin Luther King, Jr.* by David A. Adler. Illustration copyright © 1989 by Robert Casilla.

Houghton Mifflin Company: Jamaica Tag-Along by Juanita Havill, illustrated by Anne Sibley O'Brien. Text copyright © 1989 by Juanita Havill; illustrations copyright © 1989 by Anne Sibley O'Brien.

Little, Brown and Company, in association with Joy Street Books: Arthur's Pet Business by Marc Brown. Copyright © 1990 by Marc Brown. Cover and illustration from *Arthur Meets the President* by Marc Brown. Copyright © 1991 by Marc Brown.

Lothrop, Lee & Shepard Books, a division of William Morrow & Company, Inc.: Cover illustration by Carolyn Ewing from *Wake Up, City!* by Alvin Tresselt. Illustration copyright © 1990 by Carolyn Ewing.

Gina Maccoby Literary Agency: "Changing" from *Yellow Butter Purple Jelly Red Jam Black Bread* by Mary Ann Hoberman. Text copyright © 1981 by Mary Ann Hoberman. Published by Viking Penguin. "Neighbors" from *Hello and Good-By* by Mary Ann Hoberman. Copyright © 1959, renewed 1987 by Mary Ann Hoberman. Published by Little, Brown and Company.

Macmillan Publishing Company: Mitchell Is Moving by Marjorie Sharmat, illustrated by Jose Aruego and Ariane Dewey. Text copyright © 1978 by Marjorie Weinman Sharmat; illustrations copyright © 1978 by Jose Aruego and Ariane Dewey.

Vo-Dinh Mai: Cover illustration by Vo-Dinh Mai from *Angel Child, Dragon Child* by Michele Maria Surat. Illustration copyright © 1983 by Vo-Dinh Mai.

Margaret K. McElderry Books, an imprint of Macmillan Publishing Company: Friends by Helme Heine. Copyright © 1982 by Gertraud Middelhauve Verlag, Koln.

William Morrow & Company, Inc.: Old Henry by Joan W. Blos, illustrated by Stephen Gammell. Text copyright © 1987 by Joan W. Blos; illustrations copyright © 1987 by Stephen Gammell.

Orchard Books, New York: Cover illustration by Donna Rawlins from *Jeremy's Tail* by Duncan Ball. Illustration copyright © 1990 by Donna Rawlins. Cover illustration by Robert Kendall from *Mike's Kite* by Elizabeth MacDonald. Illustration copyright © 1990 by Robert Kendall.

Picture Book Studio, Ltd.: Cover illustration from *A House for Hermit Crab* by Eric Carle. © 1987 by Eric Carle Corporation.

continued on page 310

Dear Reader,

Little Penguin goes up one hill and down another in search of adventure. He discovers new places and new friends. And he learns a few important lessons along the way. Now we invite *you* to come find your own adventures!

On your journey through this book, you'll meet interesting people of different cultures and get to know exciting characters. You'll meet Mae Jemison, an African American astronaut. You'll celebrate Cinco de Mayo at a fiesta. You'll meet a group of people working together to clean up their neighborhood. The adventures you'll have will amaze you!

Through the stories, we hope you will see that we are all alike in many ways. We laugh. We get angry. We are afraid. We try our best. Come on in and read about characters like yourself. We hope you'll make a lot of new friends along the way. So open your book and come along with us.

Sincerely,
The Authors

UP ONE HILL AND DOWN ANOTHER

C O N T E N T S

Star light, star bright,
First star I see tonight,
I wish I may, I wish I might,
Have the wish I wish tonight.
Anonymous

We all have wishes and dreams. What if you could fly? What if you could be anything you want to be? You might be an astronaut! That was Mae Jemison's dream. She tried her hardest, and now she is the first African American woman astronaut. Think about *your* wishes and dreams as you read about others who say, "We can do it!"

THEMES

TRYING YOUR BEST
· ·
14

ALL ABOUT ME
· ·
44

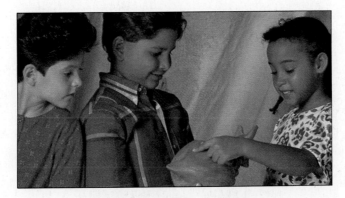

LEARNING ABOUT
EACH OTHER
· ·
70

JEREMY'S TAIL
BY DUNCAN BALL

Jeremy is at a birthday party. He is wearing a blindfold and trying his hardest to pin the tail on the donkey. But, he misses the donkey and heads out the door for an around-the-world adventure! CHILDREN'S CHOICE

HBJ LIBRARY BOOK

AUNT FLOSSIE'S HATS (AND CRAB CAKES LATER)
BY ELIZABETH FITZGERALD HOWARD

Sarah and Susan love to visit their Great-great-aunt Flossie and try on her hats. Each hat reminds Aunt Flossie of a story about interesting things she has done. ALA NOTABLE BOOK, TEACHERS' CHOICE

ARTHUR MEETS THE PRESIDENT
BY MARC BROWN

Arthur wins a writing contest! He and his class are invited to the White House so that he can say his speech to the President. Will he remember the speech? CHILDREN'S CHOICE

A PICTURE BOOK OF MARTIN LUTHER KING, JR.
BY DAVID A. ADLER

When Martin Luther King, Jr., was a boy, he loved to read and to play with his friends. When he grew up, he became a great leader. He saw things that were unfair and worked to change those things. NOTABLE CHILDREN'S TRADE BOOK IN THE FIELD OF SOCIAL STUDIES

SURPRISES
SELECTED BY LEE BENNETT HOPKINS

Poems about kids and what they do,
Dogs and wasps and subways, too!
Hopes and dreams and bugs that wiggle,
Poems in this book will make
you giggle. ALA NOTABLE BOOK,
SLJ BEST BOOKS OF THE YEAR

TRYING YOUR BEST

Have you ever tried hard to learn something new? What happened? How did you feel? In these stories, the characters have problems. But that doesn't stop them from trying their best!

C O N T E N T S

15

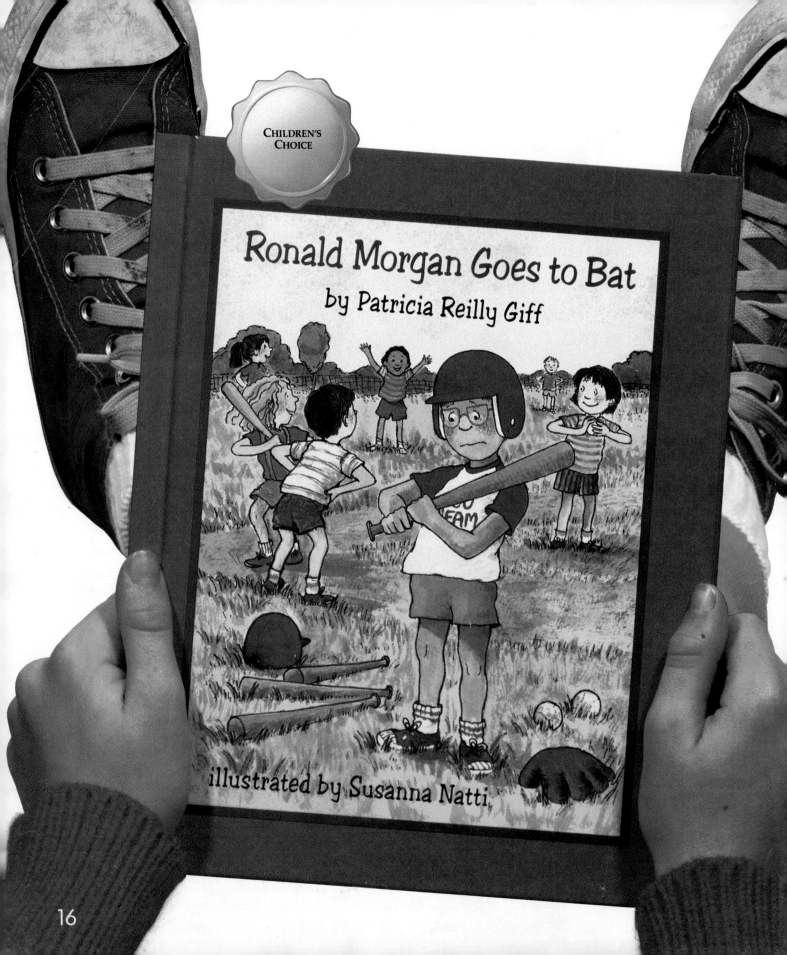

Baseball started today. Mr. Spano said everyone could play.

"Even me?" I asked.

And Tom said, "You're letting Ronald Morgan play? He can't hit, he can't catch. He can't do anything."

Mr. Spano looked at me. "Everyone," he said.

"Yahoo!" I yelled. I pulled on my red and white shirt, the one that says GO TEAM GO, and ran outside to the field.

"Two things," Mr. Spano told us. "Try hard, and keep your eye on the ball."

Then it was time to practice. Michael was up first. He smacked the ball with the bat. The ball flew across the field.

"Good," said Mr. Spano.

"Great, Slugger!" I yelled. "We'll win every game."

It was my turn next. I put on the helmet and stood at home plate.

"Ronald Morgan," said Rosemary. "You're holding the wrong end of the bat."

Quickly I turned it around. I clutched it close to the end. *Whoosh* went the first ball. *Whoosh* went the second one. *Wham* went the third. It hit me in the knee.

"Are you all right?" asked Michael.

But I heard Tom say, "I knew it. Ronald Morgan's the worst."

At snack time, we told Miss Tyler about the team.

"I don't hit very well," I said.

And Rosemary said, "The ball hits him instead."

Everybody laughed, even me.

I shook my head. "I hope it doesn't happen again."

Miss Tyler gave me some raisins. "You have to hit the ball before it hits you," she said.

We played every day. I tried hard, but the ball came fast. I closed my eyes and swung.

"If only he could hit the ball once," Rosemary said.

And Billy shook his head.

I couldn't tell them I was afraid of the ball. "Go team go," I whispered.

One day, the team sat on the grass. We watched the third grade play. They were big, they were strong, they were good. Johnny hit a home run, and Joy tagged a man out.

"We'll never hit like that," said Tom.

And Rosemary said, "We'll never catch like that either."

But I said, "Our team is the best."

Mr. Spano nodded. "That's the spirit, Ronald."

Mr. Spano told us, "Now we'll run the bases. Rosemary, you can go first."

Rosemary went fast. She raced for first base.

"Terrific, Speedy!" I yelled.

"Let me go next," I said. "I can do that, too."

But the field was muddy. My sneaker came off.

Jimmy said, "That kid's running bases the wrong way."

And Tom yelled, "Ronald Morgan. You're heading for third base."

The next day, we worked on catching. I was out in left field. While I waited, I found a stick, and started to scratch out the mud. I wrote G for go. I wrote G for great. Our team is the best, I thought. Then I wrote H for hit. H for home run. If only I could do that.

Just then I heard yelling. Someone had hit the ball.

"Catch it, Ronald!" Tom shouted.

I put down the stick. I put up my mitt. Too late. The ball sailed into the trees.

Mr. Spano took us for ice cream. "You deserve it for trying," he said. "Our team is really good."

I had a chocolate cone. Michael's a slugger, I thought. And Rosemary can really run. But I'm still afraid of the ball.

On the way home, we saw some kids playing ball.

"Want to hit a few?" Michael asked.

I shook my head. "Maybe I won't play ball anymore."

Michael said, "We need you. You have spirit. You help the team feel good."

"But how can we win?" I asked. "I can't even hit the ball."

I saw my father and ran to catch up. "See you, Michael," I said.

My father asked, "How's the champ?"

"I'm the worst," I said.

"I was the worst, too," said my father. "But then . . ."

"What?"

My father laughed. "I stopped closing my eyes when I swung."

"Maybe that's what I do."

"How about a little practice?" he asked.

We went into the yard. My father threw me some balls. I missed the first one . . . I missed the second. And then . . . I opened my eyes and swung. *Crack* went the ball.

"Ouch!" went my father. "You hit me in the knee."

"Home run!" yelled my mother.

"Sorry," I said. "Hey, I did it!"

My father rubbed his knee. "You certainly did," he said.

I ran to pick up the ball. "See you later," I said.

My father smiled. "Where are you going?"

I grabbed the bat. "Some kids are playing ball. I think I'll hit a few."

I looked back. "And you know what else? I guess I'll stay on the team. I have spirit . . . and sometimes I can hit the ball. Mike was right. I think they need me."

THINK IT OVER

1. What was Ronald Morgan's problem?

2. How did he solve his problem?

3. What things would you tell Ronald Morgan to do to become a better baseball player?

4. What do you think will happen the next time Ronald Morgan plays baseball?

WRITE

Pretend that you are Ronald Morgan. Tell a classmate how to hit a baseball. Write the steps in order.

WORDS FROM THE AUTHOR:
PATRICIA REILLY GIFF

The character of Ronald Morgan is based on a real boy. He was in one of my reading classes when I was a teacher. He never really did bad things, but he always seemed to be in some mess! He gave me the title of my first book about Ronald. I said, "I'm going to write a book about you," and he answered, "You'd better call it Today Was a Terrible Day, because that's the kind of day I'm having." So I did.

Some of my other characters are based on real people, too. Miss Tyler was my childhood piano teacher, and Mr. Spano was a gym teacher I knew when I was teaching.

My idea for <u>Ronald Morgan Goes to Bat</u> came from the time I went to camp one summer. I didn't hit the ball once the whole time we played baseball. I was a terrible player.

One reason I write for kids is to show them that most of the other children aren't stars. Ronald Morgan shows that we're all alike in some way. We all have troubles, and we all do special things. Ronald's special thing is that he's such a nice kid.

Feel good about yourself. You're special even if you're not the best reader or the best baseball player. You're important because you're you.

AWARD-WINNING
AUTHOR

POINSETTIA
and the
FIREFIGHTERS

FIRE DEPARTMENT

5

FELICIA BOND

One Saturday morning Poinsettia's father said, "Poinsettia, how would you like to have your own room? I fixed up the two rooms on the top floor, one just for you, and one just for Petunia."

Poinsettia could hardly believe her ears. That afternoon Julius and Pierre moved into her old room.

"I bet you'll be scared to sleep by yourself," Pierre snorted.

"I bet I won't," Poinsettia said.

"You can have my favorite night-light," offered Chick Pea.

"No," Poinsettia grunted. "Only babies sleep with night-lights."

Poinsettia loved her new room. She admired it all evening and into the night.

Finally her father had to call up the stairs. "Turn out your light, Poinsettia," he said. "It's way past your bedtime."

"I can't even see my hoof in front of my face," Poinsettia thought.

She opened the curtains, but there was no moonlight or starlight.

One by one the neighbors' lights went out. Poinsettia's mother and father turned off their light too. The night was very dark.

Suddenly something went CLANK!

"Petunia!" Poinsettia shouted.

"That was only your radiator," mumbled Petunia.

"I didn't see a radiator," Poinsettia said. "Are you sure I have one?" CLANK! went the sound.

"Let's invent a secret code," Poinsettia said. "If we hear a scary noise, I'll say 'peep' to make sure you're awake. Then you tell me what the noise is, okay?"

"Okay," said Petunia.

Poinsettia went back to bed.

Something creaked, v-e-r-y slowly. "Peep!" said Poinsettia.

"The stairs," said Petunia.

Something scratched, v-e-r-y roughly. "Peep!" said Poinsettia.

"A branch," said Petunia.

Something thumped, v-e-r-y loudly. "Peep!" said Poinsettia. "Peep! Peep! . . . PEEEP!"

Petunia was asleep.

"Oh, no!" Poinsettia whispered. "I am the only one awake."

She thought about the thump and the dark places where it might be.

The thump came again, and it seemed louder and closer than before. Poinsettia closed her eyes.

"Please let it be morning," she wished.

When she opened her eyes, there was a light outside. It was pink and gold.

"The sun!" Poinsettia said.

The light got bigger and brighter. But it was not sunrise.

It was a fire on the telephone wire in front of
Poinsettia's house.

"MOM!" Poinsettia shouted. "MOM! DAD!"

Poinsettia's mother called the fire department, and the entire family watched the firefighters extinguish the flames.

Afterward, three of the firefighters came into the house and filled out their report.

"You have a keen eye," one of them said to Poinsettia.

"Did the alarm wake you up?" Poinsettia asked.

"Oh, no," said the firefighter. "I'm the night watchman. I stay awake all night."

"I'm a night watcher too," Poinsettia said.

The firefighters waved good-bye.

Poinsettia went back to her room and looked out the window. The night was still dark.

Then Poinsettia saw it was not quite as dark as before.

Shining through the trees was the light from the fire station six blocks away.

"I am not the only one awake," Poinsettia said.

There were more noises that night, but they didn't bother Poinsettia.

SQUEAK

DRIP

CLATTER

And when the sun finally rose . . . Poinsettia was not awake to see it.

THINK IT OVER

1. Why couldn't Poinsettia go to sleep?

2. What happened after Poinsettia saw the bright light outside her window?

3. How did Poinsettia feel when she saw the fire station lights? Why?

4. What would you tell Poinsettia about how not to be afraid of the dark?

WRITE

What do you think will happen the next time Poinsettia tries to sleep? Add on to the story about Poinsettia. Tell what happens next.

The Tortoise and the Hare

retold by Tomie dePaola

FROM <u>TOMIE DEPAOLA'S FAVORITE NURSERY TALES</u>

Once there was a hare who met a tortoise on the road.

"How slow you are," said the hare to the tortoise.

"Not as slow as you might think," said the tortoise. "In fact, I'll challenge you to a race."

"Done," said the hare. *And that will be the easiest race I've ever won,* thought the hare.

They asked the fox to be the judge and started out. In no time at all, the hare was far ahead of the tortoise.

"I am so far ahead that I think I'll just lie down under this tree and take a nap. I'll be able to catch up to the tortoise with no trouble at all!" And the hare lay down and fell asleep.

The tortoise kept going along at a steady pace and soon passed the sleeping hare. In a little while the hare woke and rushed along but the tortoise had already crossed the finish line and won!

Moral: Slow and steady wins the race.

TRYING YOUR BEST

How are Ronald Morgan, Poinsettia, and the tortoise all alike?

. . . .

What advice might Ronald Morgan give Poinsettia about getting to sleep at night?

. . . .

WRITER'S WORKSHOP

Think about a time that you had a problem. You tried your best and solved it. Write a personal story about what happened. Tell what happened first, next, and last. You may want to draw pictures to go with your story. Then share your story with your classmates.

ALL ABOUT ME

Do you have a pet? Have you ever taken care of a pet? What happened? A lovable character named Arthur is a lot like you. In the next story, you will find out all about Arthur and the exciting things he does. Also, you'll meet Marc Brown, the writer and artist who wrote the story.

C O N T E N T S

"You've been looking at puppies for months," said D.W. "When are you going to ask Mom and Dad if you can have one?"

"I'm waiting for just the right moment," said Arthur, "so promise not to say anything!"

That night at dinner, Father asked,
"What's new?"
"Arthur wants a puppy," said D.W.
"Blabbermouth!" said Arthur.

"A puppy is a big responsibility," said Father.
"I can take care of it," said Arthur.
"We'll think about it," Mother said.
"That means no," explained D.W.

After dinner Mother and Father did the dishes.

"Can you hear what they're saying?" asked Arthur.

"They're worried about the new carpet," whispered D.W.

Suddenly the door opened. "We've decided you may have a puppy if you can take care of it," said Father.

"Wow!" said Arthur.

"*But*," said Mother, "first you need to show us you're responsible."

"How will I ever prove I'm responsible?" asked Arthur.

"The best way I know is to get a job," said D.W.

"Then you can pay back the seven dollars you owe me!"

"Ka-chingg!" went her cash register.

Arthur wondered what kind of job he could do.

"You could work for my dad at the bank," said Muffy. "He needs some new tellers."

"If I were you, I'd get a job at Joe's Junk Yard crushing old cars," offered Binky Barnes.

"Do something that *you* like," said Francine.

That gave Arthur an idea. "I'll take care of other people's pets," said Arthur, "then Mom and Dad will know I can take care of my own."

Arthur and Francine put up signs to advertise his new business. His family helped, too.

Arthur waited and waited. Then, just before bedtime, the phone rang. "Hello," he said. "Arthur's Pet Business. How may I help you?"

"Yes. No. When? Where? Great!" said Arthur.

"Hooray! I'm going to watch Mrs. Wood's dog while she's on vacation, and I'll earn ten dollars!"

"Oh, no!" said D.W. "Not nasty little Perky?"

"Isn't that the dog the mailman calls 'JAWS'?" asked Father.

"That's Perky!" said D.W.

The next morning, Arthur ran all the way to Mrs. Wood's house.

"Right on time!" said Mrs. Wood.

"*Grrrrr,*" growled Perky.

"She hasn't been herself lately," said Mrs. Wood. "I'm worried."

"I'll take good care of her," said Arthur. "We'll be best friends."

"*Grrrrr,*" growled Perky.

"Here's her schedule and a list of things she doesn't like," said Mrs. Wood. "I'll see you next Sunday."

Arthur did his best to make Perky feel at home. Every day he brushed her. He tried to fix her favorite foods. They took lots of long walks—day and night. Perky made sure they had the whole sidewalk to themselves.

"You look exhausted," said Mother. "Maybe taking care of a dog is too much work . . ."

"Any dog I get will be easier than Perky," said Arthur.

Word of Arthur's pet business got around. On Monday the MacMillans asked Arthur to watch their canary, Sunny.

On Tuesday Prunella gave Arthur her ant farm.

On Wednesday the Brain asked Arthur to take care of his frogs while he went on vacation.

Best of all, on Thursday The Amazing Larry asked Arthur to keep Cuddles, his trained boa constrictor.

Animals were everywhere—until Mother put her foot down. "I want all these animals in the basement *now!*" she ordered.

By bedtime all the pets were downstairs. All except Perky. Perky slept in Arthur's room.

On Saturday Buster asked Arthur to go to the movies.
"I can't," said Arthur. "When I finish cleaning these
cages, it will be feeding time. And anyway, it's Perky's
last night with me and she seems sick. I don't want to
leave her."

"Well, I bet you're happy today," said D.W. the next morning. "You get rid of Perky and collect ten dollars!"

"I can't believe it," said Arthur. "But I'm going to miss Perky."

"Arthur, Mrs. Wood just called to say she's on her way over," said Mother.

"Now, wait here, Perky," ordered Arthur. "I'll go and get your leash."

When Arthur went back into the kitchen, Perky was gone. "Here Perky! Perky!" called Arthur. But Perky didn't come.

"She's not in the basement," called Father.

"She's not in the backyard," said D.W.

"She's lost!" said Arthur.

"Oh, oh!" said D.W. "You're in big trouble!"

"Arthur, Mrs. Wood is here!" called Mother.

"Hi, Mrs. Wood," said D.W. "Guess what? Arthur lost Perky!"

"My poor little darling is lost?" asked Mrs. Wood.

"Don't worry," said Father. "Arthur's looking for her right now."

Suddenly they heard a bark. "Everybody come quick!" called Arthur.

"Look," said Arthur. "Perky's had puppies!"

"No wonder she's been acting so strange," said Mrs. Wood. "You've done a wonderful job taking care of Perky, when she needed a friend the most. How can I ever thank you?"

"A reward might be nice," suggested D.W.

"Shush!" said Mother.

"Here's the money I owe you," said Mrs. Wood. "And, how would you like to keep one of Perky's puppies as a special thank you?"

"I'd love to," said Arthur. "If I'm allowed."

"Of course," said Mother. "You've earned it."

"Wow!" said Arthur. "Ten dollars *and* my very own puppy! I can't believe it!"

"Neither can I," said D.W. "Now you can finally pay back my seven dollars."

"Ka-chingg!" went her cash register.

THINK IT OVER

1. What happened with Arthur's pet business from the time Arthur got Perky to the time Mrs. Wood came to take Perky home?

2. Why did Arthur start his pet business?

3. How did Arthur finally get a pet?

4. Do you think that Arthur showed that he is responsible? Why or why not?

WRITE

What will happen with Arthur and his new puppy? Write a story about Arthur and his pet. In your story, write about a problem and how the problem gets solved.

AWARD-WINNING
AUTHOR

WORDS FROM THE
AUTHOR AND ILLUSTRATOR:
MARC
BROWN

MARC

Born: November 25, 1946, Erie, PA
Home: Hingham, MA
Siblings: Three younger sisters—
Bonnie, Colleen, and Kimberly
College Attended: Cleveland Art
Institute
Jobs Held: truck driver, soda jerk,
actor, chicken farmer, TV art
director, college professor,
short-order cook, writer, and
illustrator
Married to: Laurene Krasny Brown
Children: Tolon (born 1972), Tucker
(born 1975), Eliza (born 1986)

ARTHUR

Born: sometime in 1976, Boston, MA
Home: Hingham, MA
Siblings: Two younger sisters—
D.W. (now the star of her own
series of books) and Kate (born
in the fall of 1987)
Profession: student, brother, son,
friend
Hobbies: reading, camping, magic
tricks, directing and acting,
baby-sitting
Greatest Achievement: won first
place in a writing contest and
met the President
Best Friend: Buster
Toughest Teacher: Mr. Ratburn

Many of the characters in my stories are based on my family or people I know. I grew up with three younger sisters, Bonnie, Colleen, and Kim. I based D.W. on Colleen and Kim. Bonnie was the inspiration for my character, Francine. I was afraid to tell Bonnie for a long time. She was very serious when we were growing up, and I wasn't sure how she would take the news. She is a school teacher, and I waited until I came to talk to her class to tell her. She laughed so hard, she almost fell off her chair!

The character of Buster is based on my best friend from third grade, Terry. He liked to play jokes on people, and so spent a lot of time in the principal's office. Now he's an elementary school teacher. Isn't it funny to know that a teacher was once a troublemaker?

Here's my little sister Bonnie. She's two and I'm four.

This is Arthur's little sister D.W.

I have always liked to draw. The first drawing that I can remember was one I did in second grade. I drew the Nativity scene on blue construction paper. People didn't make a fuss over it, but something happened inside me when I saw it.

My grandmother encouraged me with my drawing. She saved my artwork in her bottom drawer. My parents weren't very happy that I went to school to study art, but it was what I had always wanted to do. I taught art for a while. In 1976 the school where I was teaching closed, and I decided to follow my dream and become an artist. That was the year Arthur was born.

This is Arthur and his grandma Thora.

This is Arthur picking out glasses in <u>Arthur's Eyes</u>.

I used to wear glasses when I was in college.

Arthur is the Turkey in "The Big Turkey Hunt" in <u>Arthur's Thanksgiving</u>. Arthur also directed the play.

I played the Artful Dodger in <u>Oliver</u>. I was seventeen. I also designed the set for the play.

67

I showed my first Arthur story to an editor, and she told me that it needed a lot of work. I worked on it for six months. It's hard for me to look at that book now, because I would like to go back and do the pictures again. When you draw pictures for a book, you have to make the pictures tell the parts of the story that the words can't tell.

Now, when I'm not working on books, I'm spending my time redoing old houses on Martha's Vineyard where I live during the summer. My house is old, too. It was built in 1840. On most days, I get to my desk about 6:30 in the morning to work on books. That leaves the afternoons free to garden, to be outside working on the houses, and most importantly, to be with my family.

ALL ABOUT ME

Think about Arthur, his family, and the things Arthur did. What did you find out about Arthur?

. . . .

In what ways are Arthur and Marc Brown alike? In what ways are you like Arthur?

. . . .

WRITER'S WORKSHOP

Draw and color a picture of Arthur doing something he likes to do. Then write about the picture. Describe what Arthur looks like. Tell as much about Arthur as you can. Then share your work.

69

LEARNING ABOUT EACH OTHER

Think about the most special person you know. What makes this person so special? We are each special in some way. What makes you special? In the next story and poem, children try to learn about each other. What do they find out?

CONTENTS

I Have a Sister
My Sister Is Deaf

WRITTEN BY Jeanne Whitehouse Peterson
ILLUSTRATED BY Richard Jesse Watson

I have a sister.

My sister is deaf.

She is special.

There are not many sisters like mine.

My sister can play the piano.

She likes to feel the deep rumbling chords.

But she will never be able to sing.

She cannot hear the tune.

My sister can dance with a partner or march in a line.

She likes to leap, to tumble, to roll,

to climb to the top of the monkey bars.

She watches me as we climb.

I watch her, too.

She cannot hear me shout "Look out!"

But she can see me swinging her way.

She laughs and swings backward, trying to catch my legs.

I have a sister who likes to go with me
out to the grassy lot behind our house.
Today we are stalking deer.
I turn to speak to her. I use no voice,
just my fingers and my lips.
She understands, and walks behind me,
stepping where I step.
I am the one who listens
for small sounds.
She is the one who watches
for quick movements in the grass.

When my sister was very small,
when I went to school and she did not,
my sister learned to say some words.
Each day she sat on the floor with our mother,
playing with some toys we keep in an old shoe box.
"It's a ball," our mother would say.
"It's a dog. It's a book."
When I came home, I also sat on the floor.
My sister put her hands into the box.
She smiled and said, "Ball."
Baaaal it sounded to me.
"It's a ball," I repeated, just like our mother did.
My sister nodded and smiled.
"Ball," she said once more.
Again it sounded like *baaaal* to me.

Now my sister has started going to my school,
although our mother still helps her speak and lip-read at home.
The teacher and children do not understand every word
she says, like *sister* or *water* or *thumb*.
Today the children in her room told me,
"Your sister said *blue!*"
Well, I heard her say that a long time ago.
But they have not lived with my sister for five years
the way I have.

I understand my sister.
My sister understands what I say too,
especially if I speak slowly and move my hands a lot.
But it is not only my lips and fingers that my sister watches.
I wore my sunglasses yesterday.
The frames are very large. The lenses are very black.
My sister made me take them off when I spoke.
What do my brown eyes say to her brown eyes?
That I would really rather play ball than play house?
That I just heard our mother call,
but I do not want to go in yet?

Yes, I have a sister who can understand what I say.
But not always.
Last night I asked, "Where are my pajamas?"
She went into the kitchen and brought out a bunch of bananas
from the fruit bowl on the table.

My friends ask me about my little sister.
They ask, "Does it hurt to be deaf?"
"No," I say, "her ears don't hurt,
but her feelings do when people do not understand."

My sister cannot always tell me with words
what she feels.
Sometimes she cannot even show me with her hands.
But when she is angry or happy or sad,
my sister can say more with her face and her shoulders
than anyone else I know.

I tell my friends I have a sister
who knows when a dog is barking near her
and who says she does not like the feel of that sound.
She knows when our cat is purring
if it is sitting on her lap,
or that our radio is playing
if she is touching it with her hand.

But my sister will never know if the telephone is ringing
or if someone is knocking at the door.
She will never hear the garbage cans
clanging around in the street.

81

I have a sister who sometimes cries at night,
when it is dark and there is no light in the hall.
When I try plugging my ears in the dark,
I cannot hear the clock ticking on the shelf
or the television playing in the living room.
I do not hear any cars moving out on the street.
There is nothing.
Then I wonder, is it the same?

I have a sister who will never hear the branches
scraping against the window of our room.
She will not hear the sweet tones of the wind chimes
I have hung up there.
But when the storms come,
my sister does not wake to the sudden rolling thunder,
or to the quick *clap-clap* of the shutters in the wind.
My little sister sleeps.
I am the one who is afraid.

When my friends ask, I tell them
I have a sister who watches television
without turning on the sound.
I have a sister who rocks her dolls
without singing any tune.
I have a sister who can talk with her fingers
or in a hoarse, gentle voice.
But sometimes she yells so loud,
our mother says the neighbors will complain.

I stamp my foot to get my sister's attention,
or wave at her across the room.
I come up beside her and put my hand on her arm.
She can feel the stamping. She can feel the touching.
She can glimpse my moving hand from the corner of her eye.
But if I walk up behind her and call out her name,
she cannot hear me.

I have a sister.
My sister is deaf.

THINK IT OVER

1. What makes the little sister special?

2. How does the girl telling the story feel about her little sister? How do you know?

3. What does the little sister do for fun that you also like to do?

4. From the story, what did you learn about being deaf?

WRITE

Invite the little sister to do something fun with you. Make an invitation to give to her. Be sure to tell who, what, when, and where.

CHANGING

I know what *I* feel like;
I'd like to be *you*
And feel what *you* feel like
And do what *you* do.
I'd like to change places
For maybe a week
And look like your look-like
And speak as you speak
And think what you're thinking
And go where you go
And feel what you're feeling
And know what you know.
I wish we could do it;
What fun it would be
If I could try you out
And you could try me.

Mary Ann Hoberman

Mexican Morning
by Gg Kopilak, (1942-   )
Private Collection

LEARNING ABOUT EACH OTHER

If someone could change places with you, what would he or she be able to do?

. . . .

What do you think you could learn about someone by changing places?

. . . .

WRITER'S WORKSHOP

What makes you special? Write a personal story to tell your classmates about yourself. Tell about something that is important to you. You might tell about a time you won a prize or took a trip. Be sure to tell what happened first, next, and last. Then share your personal story.

CLASS BOOK

Mae Jemison has always tried her best. She studied hard and became a doctor. Then she joined the Peace Corps and worked in Africa because she enjoyed helping others.

Then she wanted to be an astronaut. Because of her training as a doctor and a scientist, she was chosen from a group of about 2,000 people. Mae Jemison is the first African American woman astronaut. She will go into space on one of the space shuttles.

■ Write a story about a wonderful thing you would like to do in your life. Will you be a hero? Will you have an exciting job? Will you help others? Put your story into a class book. Then dress up as yourself in the story. Tell your story to your classmates.

PLANET POSTERS

Our planet is called Earth. Read books to find out about another planet. As you read, fill in a web. Then draw a large picture of the planet, and write the information around it. Tell your classmates what you learned.

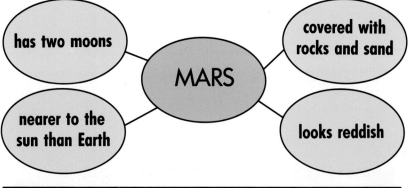

SUPER KIDS

Everyone is special! What can you do well? Work with your classmates to make a big mural. Let each person paint a picture showing something special he or she can do.

BE·A·FRIEND

Make new friends, but keep the old.
One is silver and the other gold.
Anonymous

A friend is someone you can tell a secret to. A friend makes you feel warm inside. You can play games, sing songs, and trade stories with your friends—or even put on shows! That's exactly what Luis Valdez did with his friends. Now he's a famous playwright. He writes plays that are performed all over the world. As you read this unit, think about what being a friend means to you.

CHESTER'S WAY
BY KEVIN HENKES

Chester and Wilson are best friends who have their own way of doing things. Then Lilly moves into the neighborhood. Can Chester, Wilson, *and* Lilly be friends? ALA NOTABLE BOOK

HBJ LIBRARY BOOK

FROG AND TOAD ARE FRIENDS
BY ARNOLD LOBEL

This book tells five stories about two funny friends, Frog and Toad. Like all good friends, they help each other and share many happy times. CALDECOTT HONOR, ALA NOTABLE BOOK

A HOUSE FOR HERMIT CRAB
BY ERIC CARLE

Hermit Crab is too big for his shell. So he finds a bigger shell. Through the year, he travels and meets friends who help make his home beautiful. What will happen at the end of the year? TEACHERS' CHOICE

NATHAN'S FISHING TRIP
BY LULU DELACRE

Nicholas teaches his friend Nathan how to fish. Nicholas is a mouse and Nathan is an elephant. So when they go out on a lake in a small boat, funny things happen!

ANGEL CHILD, DRAGON CHILD
BY MICHELE MARIA SURAT

Ut and her family are new to America. Her mother is still in Vietnam but will join the family soon. Ut is shy, and Raymond, a boy in her class, picks on her. Then Ut and Raymond have to work together. What will happen? NOTABLE CHILDREN'S TRADE BOOK IN THE FIELD OF SOCIAL STUDIES

MAKING NEW FRIENDS

Did you ever meet someone you didn't like and then find out that you could be friends? How did you become friends? In the next stories, characters meet each other for the first time. Will they become friends?

C O N T E N T S

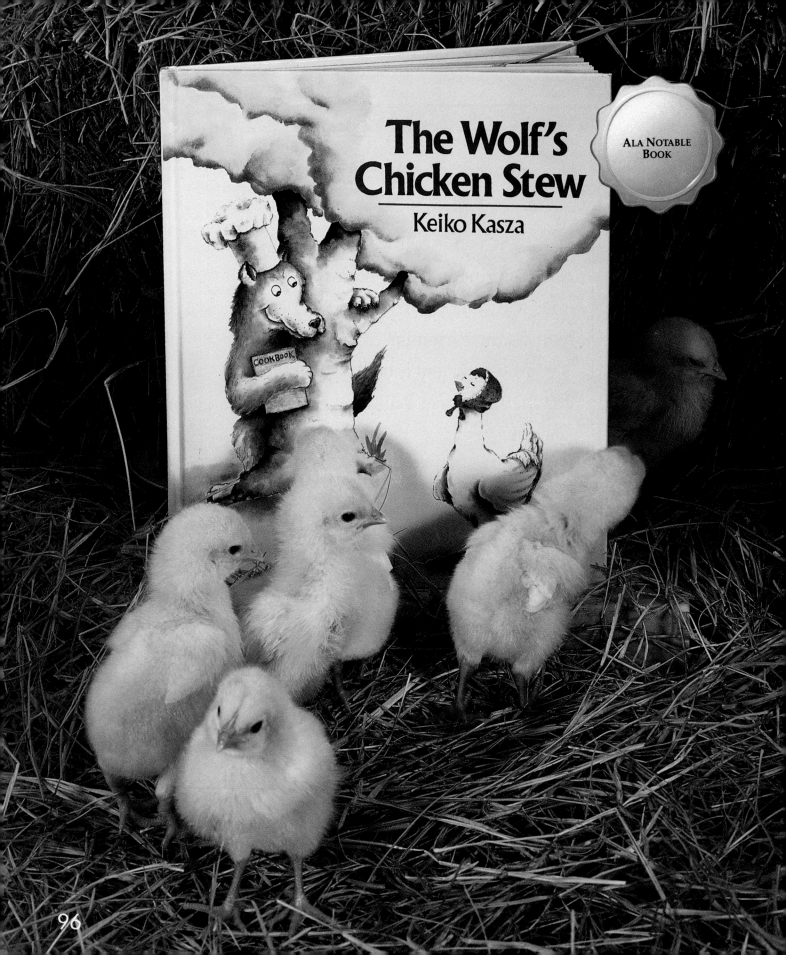

There once lived a wolf who loved to eat more than anything else in the world. As soon as he finished one meal, he began to think of the next.

One day the wolf got a terrible craving for chicken stew.

All day long he walked across the forest in search of a delicious chicken. Finally he spotted one.

"Ah, she is just perfect for my stew," he thought.

The wolf crept closer. But just as he was about to grab his prey . . .

he had another idea.

"If there were just some way to fatten this bird a little more," he thought, "there would be all the more stew for me." So. . .the wolf ran home to his kitchen, and he began to cook.

First he made a hundred scrumptious pancakes. Then, late at night, he left them on the chicken's porch.

"Eat well, my pretty chicken," he cried. "Get nice and fat for my stew!"

The next night he brought a hundred scrumptious doughnuts.

"Eat well, my pretty chicken," he cried. "Get nice and fat for my stew!"

And on the next night he brought a scrumptious cake weighing a hundred pounds.

"Eat well, my pretty chicken," he cried. "Get nice and fat for my stew!"

At last, all was ready. This was the night he had been waiting for. He put a large stew pot on the fire and set out joyfully to find his dinner.

"That chicken must be as fat as a balloon by now," he thought. "Let's see."

But as he peeked into the chicken's house . . .

the door opened suddenly and the chicken screeched, "Oh, so it was you, Mr. Wolf!"

"Children, children! Look, the pancakes and the doughnuts and that scrumptious cake—they weren't from Santa Claus! All those presents were from Uncle Wolf!"

The baby chicks jumped all over the wolf and gave him a hundred kisses.

"Oh, thank you, Uncle Wolf! You're the best cook in the world!"

Uncle Wolf didn't have chicken stew that night but Mrs. Chicken fixed him a nice dinner anyway.

"Aw, shucks," he thought, as he walked home, "maybe tomorrow I'll bake the little critters a hundred scrumptious cookies!"

THINK IT OVER

1. What happened when the wolf and the chicken finally met one another?

2. Why did the wolf leave the food at the chicken's house?

3. Do you think that the wolf expected to become friends with the chicken? Why or why not?

4. What did you think of the wolf at the beginning of the story? What did you think of him at the end?

WRITE

What did the wolf do to prepare the chicken for his stew? Write a list of the things he did.

KEIKO KASZA

AWARD-WINNING AUTHOR

I was born and raised in a very small town in Japan. In second grade, I was a bossy child, but when I was ten years old, we moved to a big city. Instead of being bossy, I became very shy.

My husband's mother gave me the idea for <u>The Wolf's Chicken Stew</u>. She is always telling me that when people are mean to you, you should be very nice to them in return.

The best thing about drawing the pictures for my own stories is that I can change anything I want. The worst thing about being both the writer and the illustrator is that I have to spend a lot of time by myself.

THE LION AND THE MOUSE

retold and illustrated
by Eve Rice

FROM
ONCE IN A WOOD: TEN TALES FROM AESOP

One day, a mighty Lion was fast
asleep in the woods. Thinking he was
just a rock, a little Mouse ran up his
back. The Lion woke at once and took
the poor Mouse by the tail.

"How dare you wake me up?" he roared. "I am going to eat you!"

"Oh, please," the Mouse said. "Let me go, and someday I will repay you."

"Don't be silly!" Lion roared. "How will you repay me? You are just a little Mouse—too small to be much use to me." But then he laughed.

"All right. Go on." He put the Mouse down and she ran off into the woods.

When many days had passed, the Mouse ran by that place again. And hearing an awful roar, she soon found Lion, caught in a trap made of rope.

Quickly Mouse ran to the trap. She took the rope in her teeth and chewed and chewed until she chewed right through the rope and set the Lion free.

"Thank you!" roared Lion.

"You are welcome," said the Mouse.

"And now I hope that you can see

how big a help small friends can be."

I Love Saturday

PATRICIA REILLY GIFF

Illustrated by Frank Remkiewicz

Saturday used to be my best day. But now there's something different. It's all because of Jessica Jeanne, the TV queen. I'll tell you all about it.

First about me. My name is Katie Cobb. *K* for Katie. *C* for Cobb. I used to do it backwards. But that was a long time ago, last year.

I have one thing, a secret. Nobody knows about it except Charles and Dexter, my mother and father, and my red cat Willie, of course. Maybe I'll tell about it later.

I live in the neatest place. It's called Greenwich Village. It has tall, gray buildings, and brown houses with stairs that go up to the second floor, and a dance studio where ballerinas practice. Car horns go *blaaaaaah*, and people bump umbrellas into each other, and have to say "excuse me," twenty times in a block. But I don't want to talk about that right now. I want to talk about Saturday.

DELICATESSEN

VILLAGE HARDWARE

10163

OPEN

On Saturdays I wake up early. I play a game of checkers by myself, and then a game of jacks. After a while I get tired of always winning so . . . I put on my skinny jeans and my shirt that says: QUIET PLEASE. I tuck a tiny piece of blanket into my pocket. (That's part of the secret.)

Then I zip down to 3B to see if Mrs. Zelinsky is up yet. She has the best sugar cookies in the world. Even Charles the doorman says so.

"It's too early, Katie," Mrs. Zelinsky always says. But she hands me a sugar cookie anyway . . . which I eat around the edges as I zoom up to the fourth floor.

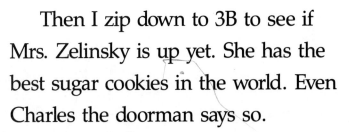

Dexter, the handyman, is painting the walls, except that he's off on Saturdays. He always leaves the can of green and a big fat brush in the corner. So I paint a tall *K* for Katie and a *C* for Cobb. Mr. Curso pops his head out of 4F.

"It's a good thing Dexter says you're his helper," he says. "Otherwise you'd be in trouble."

I help Charles stack the mail, dust the lady on
the table, and neaten up the desk.

Charles says, "I'd never get finished without you,
Katie."

I nod my head, "I know."

Then I race down Sixth Avenue to the market where John tips his straw hat at me, and wipes his hands on his long white apron. He gives me a bologna end and a slice of liverwurst for the trip back.

"How's my favorite girl?" he always asks.

But this Saturday, *this Saturday*, something terrible happened. Mrs. Zelinsky in 3B didn't even open her door.

"I gave out my last cookie," she said.

And on the fourth floor, someone had painted already. The brush was a mess and so was the floor . . . with dots all over the rug. And on the wall was a big green

And what else was: The mail was sorted, and the table with the lady was dusted, and the desk was neat as a pin. At the market, John had no bologna ends, and only half a slice of liverwurst was left.

I bumped my umbrella down the street, and came inside again. There was Willie, *my* red cat, sitting on the lap of a girl with a round face, a squished-in nose, long skinny legs with dots of green paint, and a red beaded pocketbook with a silver string. (She had sugar cookie crumbs all over her mouth.)

No fair.

I put my hands on my hips. "How come you're doing all my stuff?"

"I'm visiting my grandmother, Mrs. Zelinsky."

"Come on, Willie," I said. "Let's go upstairs."

"My name is Jessica Jeanne," she said. "I love elevators, sugar cookies, and bologna ends, and sometimes I paint."

"Come on, Willie. Let's go."

"I love to watch television. My father calls me Jessica Jeanne the TV queen."

"Come on, Willie."

"I have a checkers game, and Parchesi, and Don't Break the Ice . . . a jump rope with red plaid string . . ."

"I mean it, Willie."

"I have fourteen books on my shelf, and you know what?"

In the elevator, I pressed the button for 5, and Jessica Jeanne pressed 3, while Willie stood in the middle.

"It's no fun to play alone," said Jessica Jeanne. She leaned over. "What's in your pocket?"

"It's a secret."

"I have a blanket, too."

"You do?"

"But I'm going to stop sucking my thumb next Sunday."

"Me, too."

On Saturday I take the elevator from 5 to Jessica Jeanne at 3. First we get a sugar cookie from Mrs. Zelinsky, then on 4 we paint the wall. Downstairs we help Charles stack the mail, dust the lady, neaten up the desk.

We bump umbrellas down the street for bologna ends and liverwurst at the market.

Saturday is the best day for Jessica Jeanne and me. And Willie, my red cat, of course.

THINK IT OVER

1. How did Katie feel about Jessica Jeanne when she first met her? How did Katie feel about her at the end of the story?

2. Why did Katie's feelings about Jessica Jeanne change?

WRITE

Imagine that you spend a Saturday with Katie and Jessica Jeanne. Write a journal entry about your day. First, write the date. Then, tell what you did.

Two Friends

by Nikki Giovanni

lydia and shirley have
two pierced ears and
two bare ones
five pigtails
two pairs of sneakers
two berets
two smiles
one necklace
one bracelet
lots of stripes and
one good friendship

MAKING NEW FRIENDS

What do the wolf, Lion, and Katie learn about making friends?

· ·

What advice would Lion give to the wolf about being friends with the chickens?

· ·

WRITER'S WORKSHOP

Imagine that you are a character in the fable "The Lion and the Mouse" instead of the Mouse. How would the fable be different? Write your own fable. Remember to tell how someone learns a lesson. Then share your fable with your classmates.

GOOD FRIENDS

Have you ever moved to a new place? If so, how did you feel about leaving the old place? Maybe one of your friends has moved away. Do you think about your friends who live in other places? In the story and poem that follow, friends think about why they like each other.

CONTENTS

"I have an idea," said Mitchell,
and he got some twigs and mud.
"I have the same idea," said Margo,
and she filled her laundry bag
with more twigs and mud.

Th
thic
big
huge
gigant
and sac
"We can t
she said.

Mitchell Is Moving

written by Marjorie Weinman Sharmat
illustrated by Jose Aruego and Ariane Dewey

Mitchell ran through his house. "So long. So long, everything," he shouted.

Then he ran next door to Margo's house. "I'm moving," he said.

"Where?" asked Margo.

"Two weeks away," said Mitchell.

"Where is that?" asked Margo.

"It's wherever I will be after I walk for two weeks," said Mitchell. "I have lived in the same place for a long time. It is time for me to go someplace else."

"No!" said Margo. "You have only lived next door for fifty years."

"Sixty," said Mitchell.

"Fifty, sixty. What's the difference?" said Margo. "I want you to stay next door forever."

"I can't," said Mitchell. "I do not want to wake up in the same old bedroom and eat breakfast in the same old kitchen and brush my scales and clean my nails in the same old bathroom. Every room in my house is the same old room because I have been there too long."

"Well, maybe you are just tired of the same old friend," said Margo.

"Who is that?" asked Mitchell.

"Me," said Margo. "Maybe you look at me and think,

> 'Same Old Face.
> Same Old Tail.
> Same Old Scales.
> Same Old Walk.
> Same Old Talk.
> Same Old Margo.'"

"No," said Mitchell. "I like your face, tail, scales, walk and talk. I like you."

"I like, like, like you," said Margo.

"I like, like, like you, too," said Mitchell.

He walked to the door. "I must pack," he said.

Margo sat down in front of the door. "You can't get out," she said. "I will sit here for another sixty years."

"I still like you!" shouted Mitchell as he climbed out the window.

Margo called after him. "I will glue you to your roof. I will tie you to your front door with a thick green rope. I will tape you, paper-clip you to your house. Then I will get a gigantic rubber band and loop you to your house. I will not let you leave."

"I will unglue, untie, untape, unclip and unloop myself," said Mitchell.

Mitchell ran around his house. "I'm moving, moving, moving," he shouted.

Then he gathered up some of the slimy moss near his house and wrapped it in silver foil. "Just in case there is no slimy moss two weeks away."

Mitchell scooped up some mud from a ditch. "Maybe there is no mud two weeks away. Or no swamp water," he said as he filled a plastic bag with water from his swamp and mud from his ditch.

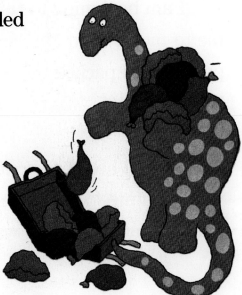

Mitchell went into his house and put the slimy moss and mud and swamp water into his suitcase.

The telephone rang. Mitchell answered it. "I will cement you to your ceiling," said Margo, and she hung up.

"I am beginning to think that Margo does not want me to move," said Mitchell as he went back to his packing. He packed the cap and mitten set that Margo had given him. "Maybe it will be cold two weeks away," he thought.

Mitchell heard a shout. He went to his window. Margo was shouting, "I will take you to the laundromat in my laundry bag, and I will wash away your idea of moving."

"Margo is a good shouter," thought Mitchell. He remembered when Margo had sent him a Happy Birthday Shout through the window:

"I'M GLAD YOU'RE THERE.
I'M GLAD I'M HERE!
HAPPY BIRTHDAY,
LOUD AND CLEAR."

"I wonder if there are any Happy Birthday Shouters two weeks away," thought Mitchell.

Mitchell held up the T-shirt that Margo had given him. It said,

MITCHELL, FRIEND OF MARGO
MARGO, FRIEND OF MITCHELL

"This shirt makes me feel sad that I am moving," said Mitchell. "But if I put it on I won't have to look at it." Mitchell put on the T-shirt. "If I don't look down at my chest, I will feel all right."

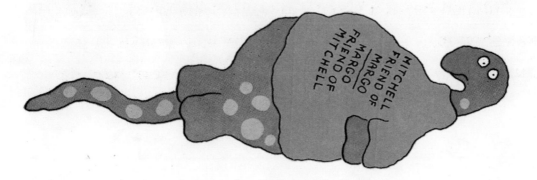

He closed his suitcase. "There. I am all packed. I am ready to go."

Mitchell walked through his house. "So long, same old rooms," he said.

Mitchell took his suitcase and went to Margo's house. "I am all ready to move," he said.

"I will stick you to your house with chewing gum," said Margo.

Mitchell picked up his suitcase and ran. "Good-by!" he called. "I will write to you every day."

Mitchell stopped running and started to walk fast. "I am a moving Mitchell," he said. Mitchell walked and walked.

When night came, he sent Margo a postcard that said,

Dear Margo,

greetings from one day away.

The second night he wrote,

Dear Margo,

more greetings from two days away.

The third night he wrote,

Dear Margo,

more and more greetings from
three days away.

"I am not much of a postcard writer," thought
Mitchell. But he sent more and more greetings to Margo
each night.

At last Mitchell reached two weeks away. "I made it!"
he said.

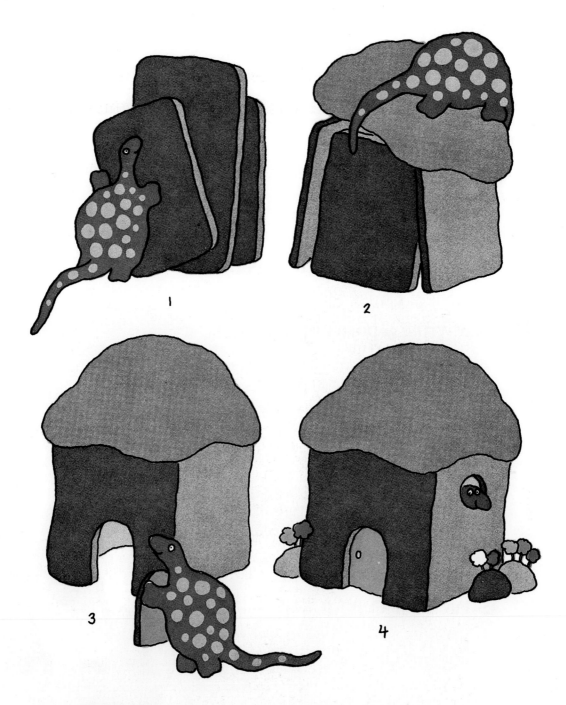

Mitchell built a house and moved in.

"I will go to bed right away so I can wake up in my new bedroom," he said.

"Mmm. New sleeps better," Mitchell said the next day.

"Now I will eat my first meal in my new kitchen. Mmm. New tastes better."

Mitchell went outside and sat down in front of his house. "This is a good house," he said. "But there is something missing. There is nobody next door. What good is a good house when there is nobody next door to it? I am lonely. I miss Margo."

Mitchell wrote a postcard to Margo:

Dear Margo,
the most greetings ever
from two weeks away.
The slimy moss is nice and slimy.
The mud is nice and thick.
The swamp water
is nice and mucky.
But I miss you.
Please come to see me.

Mitchell waited and waited. And waited.

One morning he woke up and saw a bottle of glue, a thick green rope, a big roll of tape, a huge paper clip, a gigantic rubber band, a laundry bag, a sack of cement, and a package of chewing gum. Then he saw Margo.

"Mitchell!" said Margo.

"Margo!" said Mitchell. "I am so happy to see you. Here is my new house and my new everything." Mitchell showed Margo his new house and everything around it.

"Two weeks away is terrific," said Margo as she and Mitchell ate breakfast.

"No, it isn't," said Mitchell. "There is nobody next door."

"Oh," said Margo. "I have the same problem where I am. There is nobody next door."

"I have an idea," said Mitchell, and he got some twigs and mud.

"I have the same idea," said Margo, and she filled her laundry bag with more twigs and mud. Then she got her bottle of glue, thick green rope, big roll of tape, huge paper clip, gigantic rubber band, and sack of cement. "We can use these, too," she said.

Mitchell and Margo built a house next door to Mitchell's house.

"Do you like it?" asked Mitchell.

"It's perfect," said Margo. Margo moved into her new house.

She shouted,

"I'VE COME TO STAY

TWO WEEKS AWAY.

HAPPY BIRTHDAY."

It wasn't Mitchell's birthday. But he was happy anyway.

THINK IT OVER

1. Why did Mitchell want to move? Why did Margo want him to stay?

2. How did Margo try to keep Mitchell from moving?

3. What did Mitchell not like about his new home? How did he solve this problem?

4. Do you think that Mitchell will move again? Tell why or why not.

WRITE

Imagine that you move with Mitchell. Make a list of things you will pack in your suitcase. Then tell your classmates what you will bring and why.

Reply to Someone Who Asked Why the Two of Us Are Such Good Friends

A friend doesn't have to be
Handsome or pretty.
We don't choose our friends
Just because they are witty.

My friend isn't perfect.
Others may be
Smarter or sweeter
Or nicer to me.

And sometimes we fight,
But that's quite all right—
—If we're mad in the morning,
We make up before night—
Because
        a friend
                is a friend
                        is a friend.

146

Why are we friends?
Don't ask us why.
We can't explain.
We won't even try.

Friends are not perfect.
They've plenty of flaws.
But that doesn't matter at all
Because
a friend
is a friend
is a friend.

So . . .

Whoever we are,
Whatever we be,
We're friends 'cause I'm I,
We're friends 'cause she's she.
(Or because he is he—
Whatever, whatever the case may be.)
A friend
is a friend
is a friend!

by Beatrice Schenk de Regniers
illustrations by Christoph Blumrich

148

GOOD FRIENDS

If you could ask Mitchell and Margo why they are friends, what would they say?

Could you become friends with someone like Mitchell? Why or why not?

WRITER'S WORKSHOP

Imagine that you move to a wonderful place just as Mitchell did. Make a postcard to make a classmate want to join you. On the front of the card, draw a picture of the place. On the back, write reasons why your classmate should come. Then share the postcard with your classmate.

FUN WITH FRIENDS

What are some favorite things you like to do with your friends? The next selections you will read are about friends having fun together.

Jamaica
Tag-Along

Juanita Havill

Illustrations by Anne Sibley O'Brien

Jamaica ran to the kitchen to answer the phone. But her brother got there first.

"It's for me," Ossie said.

Jamaica stayed and listened to him talk.

"Sure," Ossie said, "I'll meet you at the court."

Ossie got his basketball from the closet. "I'm going to shoot baskets with Buzz."

"Can I come, too?" Jamaica said. "I don't have anything to do."

"Ah, Jamaica, call up your own friends."

"Everybody is busy today."

"I don't want you tagging along."

"I don't want to tag along," Jamaica said. "I just want to play basketball with you and Buzz."

"You're not old enough. We want to play serious ball."

Ossie dribbled his basketball down the sidewalk. Jamaica followed at a distance on her bike.

Buzz was already at the school court, shooting baskets with Jed and Maurice.

She parked her bike by the bushes and crept to the corner of the school building to watch.

That's not fair, Jamaica thought. Maurice is shorter than I am.

Pom, pa-pom, pa-pom, pom, pom.

The boys started playing, Ossie and Jed against Buzz and Maurice.

Jamaica sneaked to the edge of the court.

Maurice missed a shot and the ball came bouncing toward her. Jamaica jumped. "I've got the ball," she yelled.

"Jamaica!" Ossie was so surprised he tripped over Buzz. They both fell down.

Jamaica dribbled to the basket and tossed the ball. It whirled around the rim and flew out.

"I almost made it," Jamaica shouted. "Can I be on your team, Ossie?"

"No. N-O, Jamaica. I told you not to tag along."

"It's not fair. You let Maurice play."

"We need two on a team. Why don't you go play on the swings and stay out of the way?"

"I still think it's not fair." Jamaica walked slowly over to the sandlot.

She started to swing, but a little boy kept walking in front of her. His mom should keep him out of the way, Jamaica thought.

She looked up and saw a woman pushing a baby back and forth in a stroller.

159

Jamaica sat down in the sand and began to
dig. She made a big pile with the wet sand from
underneath. She scooped sand from the mound
to form a wall.

"Berto help," said the little boy. He sprinkled
dry sand on the walls.

"Don't," said Jamaica. "You'll just mess it up."
Jamaica turned her back.

She piled the wet sand high. She made a castle with towers. She dug a ditch around the wall.

Jamaica turned to see if Berto was still there. He stood watching. Then he tried to step over the ditch, and his foot smashed the wall.

"Stay away from my castle," Jamaica said.

"Berto," the woman pushing the stroller said, "leave this girl alone. Big kids don't like to be bothered by little kids."

"That's what my brother always says," Jamaica said. She started to repair the castle. Then she thought, but I don't like my brother to say that. It hurts my feelings.

Jamaica smoothed the wall. "See, Berto, like that. You can help me make a bigger castle if you're very careful."

Jamaica and Berto made a giant castle. They put water from the drinking fountain in the moat.

"Wow," Ossie said when the game was over and the other boys went home. "Need some help?"

"If you want to," Jamaica said.

Jamaica, Berto, and Ossie worked together on the castle. Jamaica didn't even mind if Ossie tagged along.

THINK IT OVER

1. Why wouldn't Ossie let Jamaica play basketball?

2. Why did Jamaica tell Berto that he could help her make a bigger castle?

3. What do you think will happen the next time Jamaica wants to play with Ossie?

4. If you were Jamaica's friend, what would you do together for fun?

WRITE

Think about the lesson Jamaica learns. Pretend that Jamaica tells Ossie what she learns. Write a short play about what they say to each other.

WORDS FROM THE AUTHOR:

Juanita Havill

AWARD-WINNING AUTHOR

One of the fun things about being a writer is naming your characters. Another is choosing or making them up in the first place.

I first saw Jamaica at a park in southwest Minneapolis. I don't know her real name. I never asked her. I watched her run and jump and shout and climb on the jungle gym. I thought, "There's a girl who could be in a story." So I named her Jamaica and put her in my stories.

I love to swim and fish and ride in boats. I like cats, horses, and dogs, and I have a chubby Corgi named Victor. I take Victor on walks every day. Often on my walks I find things, especially when the snow melts in the spring. I find soggy mittens and hats, magazines and crayons and toys and watches. I always wonder who lost these items.

Writing and gardening are the two things I most like to do. Actually, writing is a lot like gardening. You start out with bare ground. Soon you have a plot full of green, growing things. Then you have to pull out all of the things that don't belong. I hope to garden and to write all of my life.

Games of Chase... Catch... Tip...

FROM THE PLAYTIME TREASURY BY PIE CORBETT

The simplest way to play touch chase is for the person who is IT to touch another player and then he or she becomes IT.

Ask some friends to play a game!

In these games, the rules are all different.

1. **Colors**
Everyone decides on a color. If you are touching that color then you are safe.

2. **Stick-in-the-Mud**
If you are touched you are frozen to the spot like a statue. When another player touches your hand, you are free.

Tiggy... Tick... Touch... It... Tag...

3.

Ticky Leapfrog

If you are touched, you crouch down. When someone leapfrogs over you, you are free.

4. Shadow Tick

This time you catch someone by touching her shadow with your foot. It doesn't count if you touch *her* at all!

5. Tunnel Touch

When you are caught, put one arm against something to make a tunnel. If someone else runs under your arm, you are free.

6. Three-Squat Tag

If you are about to be caught, you can bob down and touch the ground. Then you are safe. But you can only do this three times in a game!

Every morning, when Charlie Rooster strutted into
the barn to wake the other animals, Johnny Mouse and
fat Percy went with him to help. "Good friends always
stick together," they said. When this job was done, they
wheeled their bicycle out of the barn and set off for
their morning ride.

They could ride down the roughest paths and up the
steepest cliffs. No curve was too sharp for them and
their bicycle. No puddle was deep enough to stop them.

One day, they played a game of hide-and-seek by the village pond.

While Johnny Mouse was hiding, he discovered an old boat lying in the tall grass. He showed his friends, and they decided to play pirates. "Good friends always decide things together," they said.

Johnny Mouse took the tiller, Charlie Rooster opened his wings to make the sail, and fat Percy plugged up the hole in the side of the boat by sitting on it.

They sailed out on the open water, and as the day went on, they felt very brave and bold. They conquered the village pond!

But hunger finally sent them back to the shore.

First they tried to catch a fish. But their stomachs rumbled so loudly that they frightened all the fish away.

Then they went looking for cherries. They shared them: some for Johnny Mouse, some for Charlie Rooster, and twice as many for fat Percy.

Johnny Mouse didn't mind, but Charlie Rooster complained. He said it was unfair. So they gave him the cherry stones. "Friends are always fair," they said.

They ate so many cherries that they all got stomachaches and had to sit down for a while before they started back.

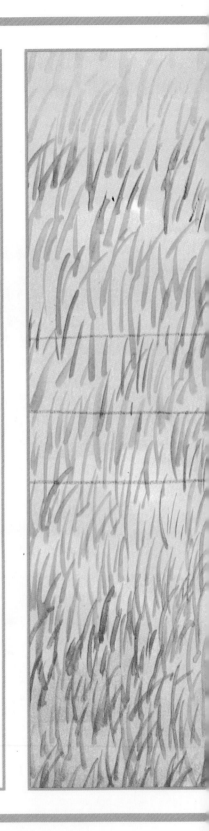

As evening fell and the shadows grew longer, they bicycled home.

Behind the henhouse, near the water barrel, they swore to be friends forever.

"Good friends always stick together," they said.

They decided to spend the night in Johnny Mouse's house. But Charlie Rooster got stuck in the doorway.

Then fat Percy invited them to spend the night with him; but Johnny Mouse said he didn't want to sleep in a pigsty.

Finally, Charlie Rooster suggested sleeping in the henhouse. They tried to rest on a perch high above the ground . . . but it broke.

So, sadly, they said good night to each other and went to their own beds. "Sometimes good friends can't be together," they said.

But that night they dreamed about each other, the way true friends do.

THINK IT OVER

1. How do you know that Charlie Rooster, Johnny Mouse, and fat Percy are friends?

2. What things did the friends do that show that they always stick together?

3. Do you think that the way the friends shared the cherries was fair? Tell why or why not.

4. Why couldn't the friends spend the night together?

WRITE

"Good friends always decide things together," the friends said. Write another friendship rule. Draw a picture to go with it. Put your page into a class book.

We're Racing, Racing down the Walk

We're racing, racing down the walk,
Over the pavement and round the block.
We rumble along till the sidewalk ends—
Felicia and I and half our friends.
Our hair flies backward. It's whish and whirr!
She roars at me and I shout at her
As past the porches and garden gates
We rattle and rock
On our roller skates.

Phyllis McGinley
illustration by Tomie dePaola

AWARD-WINNING
AUTHOR

FUN WITH FRIENDS

Which of the activities you read about would you most want to do? Why?

. . . .

How would Charlie Rooster, Johnny Mouse, and fat Percy tell Ossie to treat Jamaica?

. . . .

WRITER'S WORKSHOP

Imagine that you spend the day with Jamaica or with Charlie Rooster, Johnny Mouse, and fat Percy. What do you do for fun? Write a story about what happens. Be sure that your story has a beginning, a middle, an ending, and a title. Then share your story.

CONNECTIONS

PLAYS

When Luis Valdez was young, his family moved from place to place to do farm work. Each time they moved, Luis had to make new friends. One way that he made friends was to make up and put on exciting plays.

By the time Luis had grown up, he was sure that he wanted to keep writing plays. He started a group called Teatro Campesino. He taught the farm workers in the group how to act out stories about their lives. They became good friends who learned a lot from each other. In time, they performed all over the world.

■ Work with a group to make up a play that tells something important about your lives. Put on your play for your classmates.

WHAT SHALL WE PLAY?

Luis Valdez liked to put on plays with friends. List games your classmates like to play with friends. Then have everyone vote for his or her favorite game. Show the votes on a pictograph.

Favorite Games							
Kickball	Tony	Alison	Rosa	Jamal	Mai	Matt	Ari
Tag							
Jump Rope							
Basketball							

IT'S SHOW TIME!

With a group, read a folktale or a story about friends. Together, plan how to act out the story for your classmates. Make costumes. Practice. Then put on your show!

UNIT THREE

NEIGHBORHOODS

Some neighborhoods are quiet. Some are filled with noise and excitement. What is your neighborhood like? In many Native American neighborhoods of long ago, the sounds of music and singing filled the air when they celebrated the beauty and importance of nature. Today, Native Americans still celebrate. Think about how your neighborhood is like the neighborhoods you read about in this unit.

BOOKSHELF

MIKE'S KITE
BY ELIZABETH MacDONALD

One day a big wind blows Mike
and his kite up into the air.
"Help! Help!" he cries. Many
people and animals try to pull
him down as he flies across town.

HBJ LIBRARY BOOK

DONNA O'NEESHUCK WAS CHASED BY SOME COWS
BY BILL GROSSMAN

Donna O'Neeshuck is chased through town
by some cows. She is also chased by chickens,
bears, a herd of buffalo, and a policeman!

Find out why they all want
to catch Donna O'Neeshuck.

CHILDREN'S CHOICE

ONCE AROUND THE BLOCK
BY KEVIN HENKES

Annie is bored. She has no one to play with and nothing to do. Her mother says she should take a walk around the block. On her walk, Annie finds some nice surprises. AWARD-WINNING AUTHOR

WAKE UP, CITY!
BY ALVIN TRESSELT

The sun has just come up, and ducks begin to call to one another. A huge ship comes into the dock. Babies cry for breakfast. Find out what else happens as a city wakes up. NOTABLE CHILDREN'S TRADE BOOK IN THE FIELD OF SOCIAL STUDIES

HILL OF FIRE
BY THOMAS P. LEWIS

A farmer is upset because nothing interesting ever happens in his village. Each day is like the next. But one day when he plows his field, he gets a big surprise! READING RAINBOW BOOK

THEME

LET'S BE NEIGHBORS

Do people in your neighborhood get along with one another? Do you play with your neighbors or invite your neighbors over to your home? The next stories you will read are about two sets of neighbors and what they do.

CONTENTS

JUNK DAY
on Juniper Street

written by Lilian Moore
illustrated by Eric Hanson

FROM JUNK DAY ON JUNIPER STREET

DAVY'S FATHER

DAVY

DAVY'S MOTHER

How did it begin? No one on Juniper Street can really say. Benny and Jenny say it began in their house. Debby says it really began in her backyard. But Davy thinks his father started it all.

One morning Davy's father was reading his newspaper.

"Take a look at this!" he said to Davy's mother.

DO YOU HAVE JUNK
AROUND *YOUR* HOUSE?
THEN IT'S CLEAN-UP TIME!

"Do we have junk?" asked Davy.
"Well . . ." said his mother.

191

Later, Davy's mother and Debby's mother met in the backyard. Davy's mother said, "Look at this." And she showed her the newspaper.

DO YOU HAVE JUNK

AROUND *YOUR* HOUSE?

THEN IT'S CLEAN-UP TIME!

"Do *we* have junk?" asked Debby.

"Hmmmmmm . . ." said her mother.

Later, some mothers met to have coffee. They met at Benny and Jenny's house. "Did you see this?" asked Debby's mother. And she showed them the newspaper.

Jenny asked, "Do *we* have junk?"

All the mothers began to laugh.

"We all have junk," they said. "Lots and lots of junk!"

Then someone said, "Let's do it! Let's have a Take-Out-All-the-Junk-Day!"

DEBBY'S MOTHER

DEBBY

DEBBY'S FATHER

DAVY'S FATHER

DAVY

JENNY'S MOTHER

JENNY

So Juniper Street had a Junk Day. It was a big clean-up time in every house. Mothers and fathers and children walked from one room to the next, saying, "Do we need *this* anymore? Do we want to keep *that?*"

Then everyone began to put out the junk
- the old chairs
- the old tables
- the old toys and pictures and books.

And every time they looked around the house, people saw more junk to take out
- an old lamp
- a yellow bird cage
- a big old rocking chair.

194

Soon there was a pile of junk outside every house on Juniper Street.

Davy's father looked up and down the street.

"Wow!" he said. "We will need a big truck to take all this away!"

Benny's father called up the junk man. "We have lots of junk on Juniper Street," he told the man. "You will need a big truck to take it all."

"I have a big truck," said the junk man. "But I can't come today. I will come for your junk in the morning."

"Don't forget," said Benny's father. "A big truck."

All day, people walked past the piles of junk on Juniper Street. It was hard to go by without taking a good look.

Davy stopped outside Debby's house. "Say, there's a good wheel!" he cried. "I need a wheel like that for my wagon. May I have it?"

Debby's mother said yes.

Later Debby's father stopped to look at the junk outside Davy's house. He saw an old tool box. "Why, it's just what I need!" he said.

"Take it!" said Davy's father.

Soon many people were saying, "Take it!"

Jenny's mother saw a little table she liked. "I need a little table in the little room," she said.

Debby's mother found a big hatbox in the junk outside Jenny's house. "I can keep my big red hat in this," she said happily.

Jenny saw a doll bed across the street. She took her doll Amanda across the street and put her in the bed. "It's just like the three bears," she told Amanda, "not too big, not too little, but just right!" So Jenny asked for the doll bed.

DAVY

DEBBY

DEBBY'S MOTHER

JENNY'S MOTHER

JENNY

JUNIPER

MA[IN]

BUS STOP

197

By this time everyone was visiting the junk next door and the junk across the street.

A man picked up a lamp. "Do you call *this* junk?" he said. "I can fix this lamp in no time." And off he went with it.

An old lady took home the yellow bird cage. "Now I can get a bird!" she cried.

Someone was happy to find a window box. "I'll paint it green," he said, "and put in some red geraniums."

Someone saw an old picture of the sea. "I lived by the sea when I was a boy," he said, and he took the picture home.

By the time the sun went down, there was no more junk on Juniper Street—well, almost none.

One thing was left.

It was a big rocking chair. Many people stopped to look at it, but everyone said, "Too big!" So there it stood.

The next morning a big truck came down Juniper Street.

"Oh my," said Benny's father. "We forgot to tell the junk man not to come!"

The truck came slowly down the street and stopped. The man who got out of the truck was big, too. He looked up and down the street. All he saw was the rocking chair. He walked over and looked at it. Then he sat down and began to rock. "At last!" he said happily. "A big rocking chair!"

199

Then he put the chair on his truck, and off he went with all the junk on Juniper Street.

THINK IT OVER

1. What was the reason for Junk Day?

2. At the end of the day, did the houses on Juniper Street have any junk in them? Explain your answer.

3. What was the last piece of junk left on Juniper Street? Who took it?

4. Have you ever found something useful that someone else thought was junk? Tell about it.

WRITE

Make a poster announcing a junk day on your street. Write the date, time, and reason for your junk day. Draw pictures on your poster.

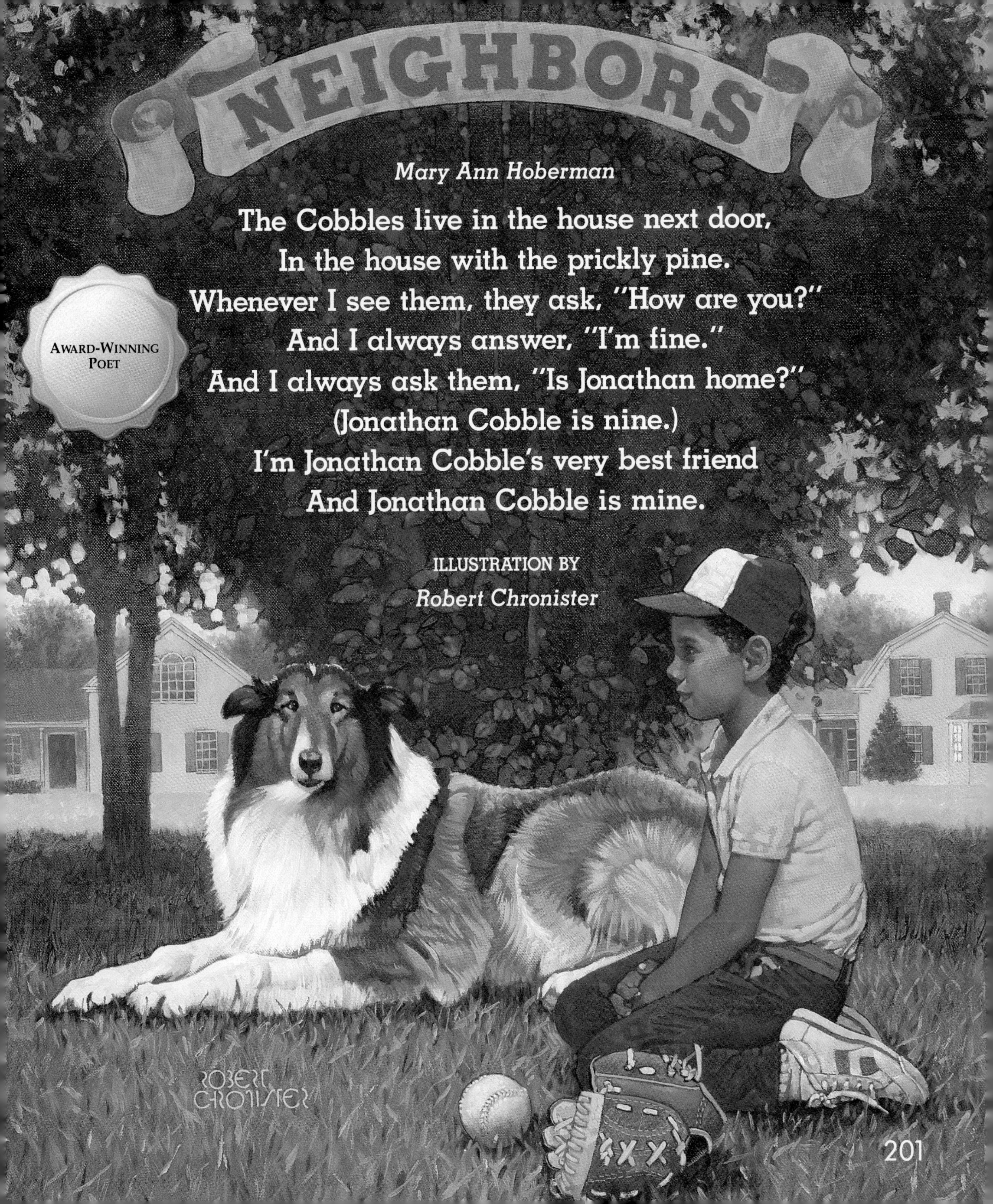

NEIGHBORS

Mary Ann Hoberman

AWARD-WINNING
POET

The Cobbles live in the house next door,
In the house with the prickly pine.
Whenever I see them, they ask, "How are you?"
And I always answer, "I'm fine."
And I always ask them, "Is Jonathan home?"
(Jonathan Cobble is nine.)
I'm Jonathan Cobble's very best friend
And Jonathan Cobble is mine.

ILLUSTRATION BY

Robert Chronister

JOAN W. BLOS

O·L·D H·E·N·R·Y

ILLUSTRATED BY
STEPHEN GAMMELL

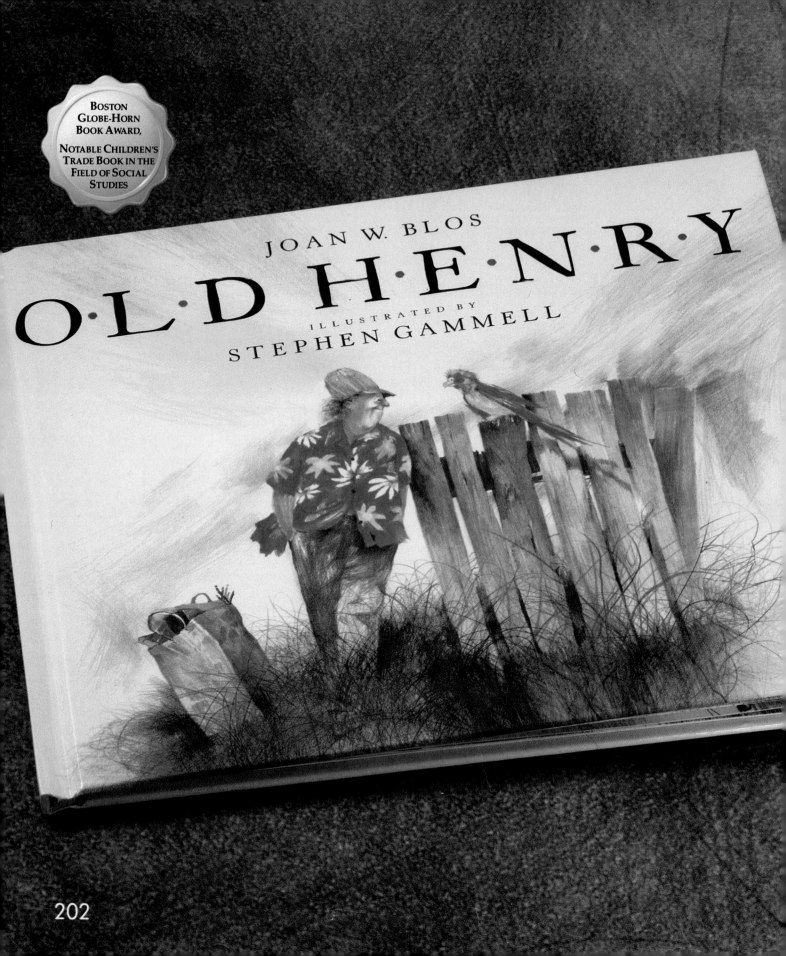

The story begins when a stranger appears
and moves into a house that was vacant for years.

No one thought he meant to stay;
the house was drafty, dark and gray,
and more than seven years had passed
since anyone had lived there last.

HOUSE
FOR
RENT

He meant to stay.

He had no doubt.
It suited him from inside out,
and in its vast and dusty spaces
all the things he had
found places.

That Henry!

The neighbors watched him moving in
and promised each other he'd soon begin
to fix things up a bit.

He did not think of it.

With money enough to pay the rent,
his books, birds, and cooking pots,
he was content
and never did notice (or else didn't care)
that people whispered everywhere:

"That place
is a disgrace."

"At least," they remarked, "you would think that he could show a little respect for the neighborhood."

"That place is a disgrace."

At last they decided to form a committee
and went to him saying, "We are proud of our city.
If you'd only help out, think how good it would look—"
"Excuse me." He bowed,
and went back to his book.

That Henry.

Then they fined him fines. They threatened jail.
They wrote him long letters and sent them by mail:

"Dear Henry . . ."

Still the hollyhocks wilted, unwatered, unkept;
the gatepost stayed crooked, the walk stayed unswept.
And things went on as they'd begun,
and he angered his neighbors, one by one.

"So unfriendly!"
"Never talks!"

"Can't we *make* him sweep his walks?"
"No, there's nothing we can do—
You nasty Polly! Shoo, bird, shoo!"

On a day in November they sought the advice
of the mayor, who suggested being nice.

"Being *nice*?"
"Please,
try it twice."

But when two of the ladies baked him a pie,
he said, "I'm not hungry. No, thank you. Good-bye."
And when three of the men said they'd shovel his snow,
he quickly said: "No!"

"We told you so!"

Now Henry, too, had had his fill.
That night he grumbled, "I never *will*
live like the rest of them, neat and the same.
I am sorry I came."

Then he packed some things in shopping bags
and tied the rest in three old rags.

He didn't make plans, he just left a short note, a
hastily written: G o n e t o D a k o t a.

He taped it to the big front door.

And no one lived there

anymore.

His day lilies bloomed; his phlox grew tall.
They picked his apples in the fall.

They picked his apples, and now and then
someone would ask, "Remember when . . .?
                    Remember when . . .?
                    Remember when . . .?"

Later still, in winter's snow,
they asked one another, "Where did he go?"
"Will he come again?"
"His house looks so empty, so dark in the night."
"And having him gone doesn't make us more right."

That Henry.

"Maybe, some other time, we'd get along
not thinking that somebody *has* to be wrong."
"And we don't have to make such a terrible fuss
because everyone isn't exactly like us."

Meanwhile, Old Henry, to his great surprise,
was missing the neighbors who'd brought him the pies.
In spite of their nagging, he really did care
for them and their street. So he wrote to the mayor:

Dear Mr. Mayor,

I am finding it hard
to be far from my house
and my tree and my yard.

If I mended the gate,
and I shoveled the snow,
would they not scold my birds?
Could I let my grass grow?

Please write and tell me
the answers, so then we
can all get together.

Sincerely yours,

Henry

THINK IT OVER

1. Why didn't Henry and his neighbors get along?

2. How did the mayor ask the neighbors to treat Henry?

3. What lesson did Henry and his neighbors learn?

4. What else could the neighbors have done to get along with Henry?

WRITE

Pretend you are the mayor. Write a letter to Henry to answer his questions.

LET'S BE NEIGHBORS

If Henry moves back into his house, do you think that he and his neighbors will have a junk day? Why or why not?

· ·

Do you think that Henry would like to live on Juniper Street? Do you think that the people on Juniper Street would like Henry? Tell why you think as you do.

· ·

WRITER'S WORKSHOP

Write a friendly letter to Henry or to one of the children on Juniper Street. Tell that person about your neighborhood. Also, tell your ideas for making Henry's neighborhood or Juniper Street a better place to live. Then send your letter to a classmate.

ADVENTURES NEAR AND FAR

Think about a time when you were by yourself and farther from home than you had ever been before. Were you excited? Did you feel brave? Read about a penguin exploring far from home.

C O N T E N T S

Little Penguin's Tale

written and illustrated by
AUDREY WOOD

CHILDREN'S
CHOICE

Shhh, little penguins. Now don't make a peep, and Grand
Nanny Penguin will tell you a tale of long, long ago.

Once there lived a little penguin just like you. Just like you,
except Little Penguin didn't listen to his Grand Nanny's tales.

One morning, at the break of dawn, he snuck off by himself to find some fun in the snowy, polar world.

Up one hill and down another, he soon left all his friends behind.

"Look at me!" Little Penguin cried. "I'm sliding on my tummy far, far away from home!"

Now everyone knows a little penguin can get lost far, far away from home.

223

But he didn't.

Right away, Little Penguin came upon a band of dancing gooney birds. They were beating on tin cans and blowing tunes through empty glass bottles.

Little Penguin had never heard such music. It tickled his beak and made him laugh. His feet began to move.

"Look at me!" Little Penguin cried. "I'm dancing with the gooney birds!"

Now everyone knows a little penguin can get into big trouble dancing with the gooney birds.

225

But he didn't.

Soon they all danced into a rickety boat and sailed out to the Walrus Polar Club.

"Jolly good, old chaps!" a walrus called. "Do come in and have some fun, won't you?"

"Hey, ho!" the gooney birds cheered. "We will."

"Me, too!" Little Penguin said, and he followed them inside.

Little Penguin had never seen such a place. It was a madcap club where animals gathered from all over the world to do whatever they pleased.

Before long, he jumped in the middle and joined the fun. "Look at me!" Little Penguin cried. "I'm the wildest of them all!"

Now everyone knows a little penguin can get hurt
when he's the wildest of them all.

But he didn't.

On and on they danced and played until even the
wildest grew weary. Little Penguin could hardly keep his
eyes open. So he wandered outside and lay down to take
a nap.

"Look at me!" Little Penguin yawned. "I'm falling
asleep by the deep, dark sea."

Now everyone knows a little penguin can get eaten by a whale if he falls asleep by the deep, dark sea.

And that's just what happened.

A great whale opened its mouth and gobbled him up in one bite.

Poor Little Penguin. That was the end of him.

Oh, dear! My goodness! Don't cry, little penguins. It's just a tale of long ago. And . . . I suppose it could have ended differently.

Now where was I? Ahhh, yes. Little Penguin fell
asleep by the deep, dark sea. Then a great whale opened
its mouth and tried to gobble him up.

But Little Penguin was too clever. Quick as a wink,
he jumped out of the whale's mouth, into the rickety
boat . . .

and sailed all the way back home to his Grand Nanny
and friends. But not, mind you, before the great whale
managed to nip off a few of his very best tail feathers.

And that is the end of Little Penguin's tale.

THINK IT OVER

1. What do you think Little Penguin learned from his adventures?

2. Why did Little Penguin sneak off at dawn?

3. Why do you think Grand Nanny Penguin changed the ending to her tale?

4. What would you say to Little Penguin about looking for fun far from home?

WRITE

Grand Nanny Penguin told two endings to the story of Little Penguin. Write a third ending for the story.

Words from the Author and Illustrator: AUDREY WOOD

AWARD-WINNING AUTHOR

My ideas for Little Penguin's Tale came from a couple of different places. On a trip to Sea World in San Diego, I visited the Penguin Encounter. I drew lots of sketches of the penguins swimming and playing.

The penguins interested me so much that I began reading a lot about them. I learned that young penguins are cared for by penguin nannies while their parents look for food. That gave me the idea for Grand Nanny Penguin.

Now that I knew what to write about, it was time to learn more. I read all about the South Pole. I even went back to Sea World to spend time with the penguins inside the Penguin Encounter. The best part was being allowed to hold a baby penguin in my arms.

Back home, I started drawing the penguins from memory. I couldn't picture how their shadows would fall on snow. So I built a model of the South Pole out of plaster of Paris. I put little papier-mâché penguins on it. Then I shone a light over my model to make shadows. As I moved the light, the shadows changed. Now I understood how to make my drawings in Little Penguin's Tale begin in the morning and end at night. Look and see how the penguins' shadows and the colors of the sky change from the beginning of the story to the end.

STEP 1 ONE

Gather the things you will need.

Little Penguin Puppet

Little Penguin left his neighborhood to find adventure. You can help him find more adventure by making a Little Penguin hand puppet. Follow these directions to make your puppet.

STEP 2 TWO

With your crayons, draw a penguin face on the white paper.

STEP 3 THREE

Wrap the paper around and glue the edges together. Make sure the face is on the outside.

STEP 5 FIVE

Cut out the wings and glue them on your penguin.

STEP 4 FOUR

Fold the black paper in half. Place the pattern on the fold and trace two wings.

STEP 6 SIX

Cut a small triangle out of black paper. Glue the black triangle to the back of your penguin to form a tail.

STEP 7 SEVEN

Cut webbed feet out of orange paper. Fold up the edge of the feet. Place glue on the edge.

STEP 8 EIGHT

Glue the feet to the bottom of your penguin. When you are finished, your penguin hand puppet may look like this.

Place your hand inside your puppet. Move your hand to make Little Penguin move. Use your voice to speak for Little Penguin. Pretend that you are Grand Nanny Penguin as you make up your own Little Penguin tales.

ADVENTURES NEAR AND FAR

How did Little Penguin have fun far from home? What fun things could he learn to do close to home?

. . . .

What if "Little Penguin's Tale" were about a child instead of a penguin? What kinds of adventures would that child have?

. . . .

WRITER'S WORKSHOP

Think about an adventure that you had when you were with someone older than you. Write an exciting story about your adventure. Be sure your story has a beginning, a middle, an ending, and a title. You may want to add pictures or photographs to your story. Then share your adventure story.

SPECIAL TIMES

Does your neighborhood ever have a parade or a picnic or some other special event? The next stories you will read are about special things that happen in two neighborhoods.

C O N T E N T S

FIESTA!

CINCO DE MAYO
by June Behrens

We hear music, music everywhere. We sing and dance and eat and play. The fiesta in our park is like a big party. Welcome to the fiesta!

Many people wear bright and beautiful Mexican costumes. Look at the sombreros Joe and his friends are wearing. A sombrero is a hat with a very broad brim. It is almost as big as little Joe.

This is a Cinco de Mayo fiesta party. Cinco de Mayo means fifth of May. The fifth of May is a joyous festival day, a very special day for Mexican Americans. It is an important day for all the people in America.

On May 5, 1862, there was a big battle in the town of Puebla, Mexico. In a battle with the French army, the poor, ragged Mexican army won a great victory.

The victory helped to drive foreigners out of North America. No foreign power has invaded North America since. Each year, on the fifth of May, people celebrate the victory of Cinco de Mayo.

On the great outdoor stage in our park, dancers in ruffled skirts clap their hands. The music is fast and exciting. The dancers stamp their feet and whirl around. We sit on the hillside and watch the show.

Musicians walk around our park. They play their guitars and violins and trumpets. They are called mariachi musicians. When they sing, they give a happy little yell. *Yi . . . Yi . . . yiyyyyyyyyy!*

There are good smells everywhere. Mothers and fathers make tortillas in the food stand. Tortillas look like thin, flat pancakes. Father folds the tortilla in the middle and fills it with beans and lettuce and tomatoes. Sometimes he adds hot sauce, too.

On stage, little señoritas and their partners dance for us. The mariachis play. Everyone claps and sings the lively song.

At school everyone joins in the Cinco de Mayo holiday fiesta. We decorate our school with the colors of the Mexican flag—green, red, and white. We hang the flag outside.

We have Cinco de Mayo contests and games. The most fun of all is the taco-eating contest!

We decorate our fiesta booths with Mexican tissue paper flowers. We take turns playing with Mexican toys and games. We even dig for Mexican archeological treasures.

We make flour tortillas. We mix flour, salt, and baking powder together. Then we add oil and water. We make little dough balls and roll them out flat. Then we cook them in a pan. Delicious!

Fathers and mothers come to see our Cinco de Mayo programs. We sing Mexican songs and do special dances. Our mothers and fathers like the beautiful Mexican murals we have painted.

All day and into the evening we celebrate Cinco de Mayo. We have a piñata party in the evening. The piñata is a clay pot decorated with bright-colored tissue paper. Piñatas are made in many shapes and sizes. Our piñata is a giant star. It is filled with candy!

The piñata hangs from a rope above the heads of boys and girls. Joe is blindfolded and given a stick. He swings again and again at the hanging piñata. At last he hits it. Candies fly everywhere and scatter on the ground. Everyone scrambles for a piece.

Cinco de Mayo is over until next year. Our Mexican American friends have taught us songs and games. They have taught us dances and Spanish words. *Amigo* means friend. Everyone has been a good amigo on Cinco de Mayo.

Viva la fiesta!

THINK IT OVER

1. Why is the fifth of May such a special day?

2. What do you think Mexico would be like today if the Mexican army had lost the battle?

3. Have you ever seen or done any of the things that happen at the fiesta? If so, tell about them.

4. How are flour tortillas made?

WRITE

Suppose that your class will make a piñata to celebrate Cinco de Mayo. Write a list of everything you will need and the directions for making the piñata.

CELEBRATION

I shall dance tonight.
When the dusk comes crawling,
There will be dancing
   and feasting.
I shall dance with the others
   in circles,
      in leaps,
         in stomps.
Laughter and talk
   will weave into the night,
Among the fires
   of my people.
Games will be played
And I shall be
   a part of it.

Alonzo Lopez

illustration by Tomie dePaola

257

Miss Eva
and the
Red Balloon

by Karen M. Glennon

illustrated by
Hans Poppel

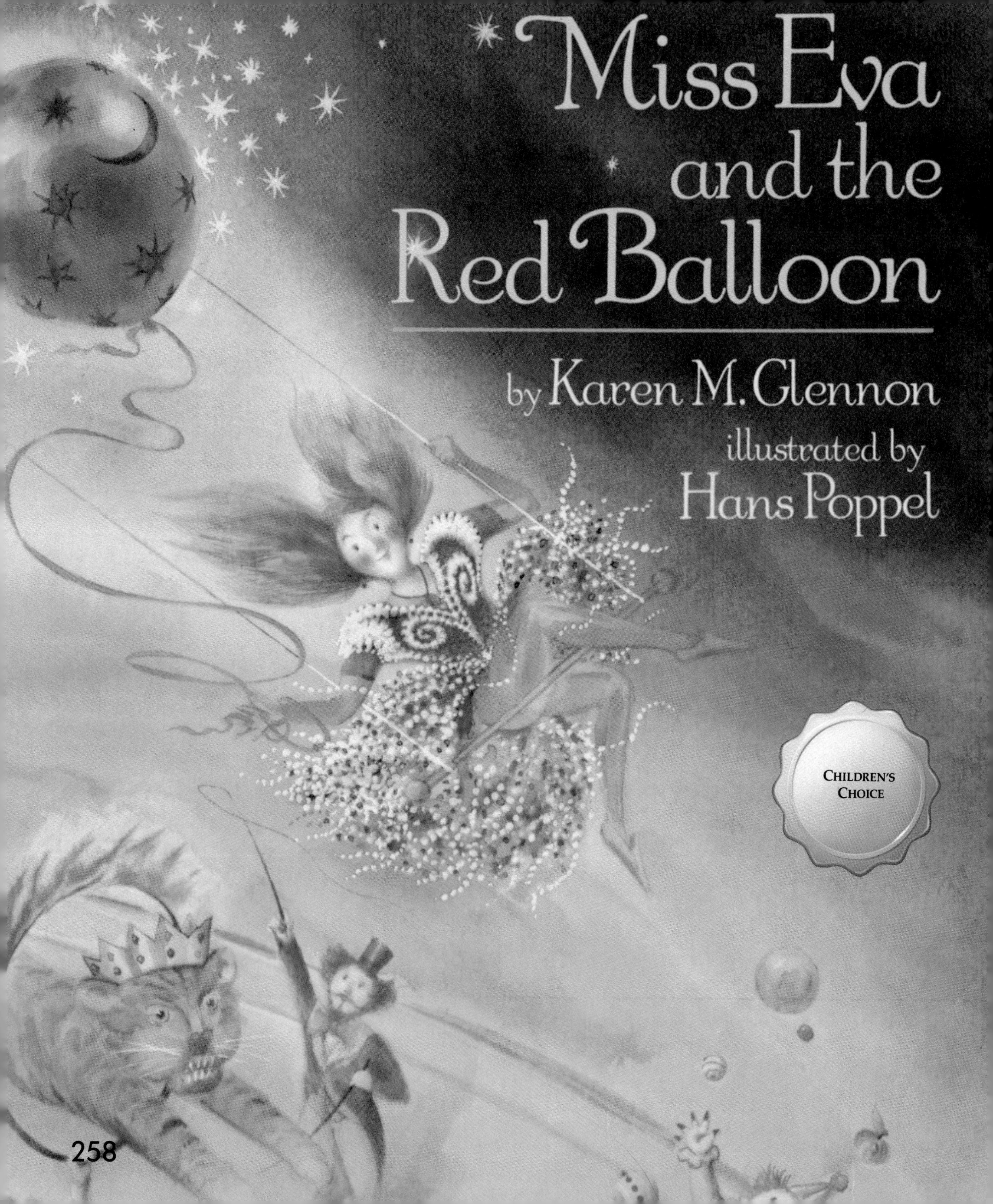

CHILDREN'S
CHOICE

That day Miss Eva wore the same black dress she wore every day. She left her house at 7:22, just as she did every day.

She passed Spencer's Market and waved to Mr. Spencer, just as she did every day. She walked across the street while Mike the policeman held the traffic, just as he did every day. She walked up the steps of Greenbrier Elementary School, just as she did every day. She taught second grade, just as she did every day.

But after Adam Sumner's birthday party, everything changed!

Adam's father brought colored balloons for
everyone. They were round helium balloons tied with
shiny ribbons.

When Adam went home, he gave
Miss Eva his favorite balloon. It was
red with green stars and moons.

After everyone had gone, Miss Eva got ready to go
home. When she tried to put on her hat, she was surprised.
Her hand wouldn't let go of the ribbon! Miss Eva had to
leave her best hat at school.

Mike the policeman said, "Nice day, Miss Eva," just as he always did.

Miss Eva nodded her head, just as she always did. She hurried across the street, just as she always did. But today she had the red balloon in her hand.

At Spencer's Market, Joe said, "Nice tomatoes today, Miss Eva."

But Miss Eva had Adam Sumner's red balloon in her hand. She just shook her head and kept walking.

Mike the policeman and Mr. Spencer both noticed something different about Miss Eva.

Miss Eva's house looked the same as always. Miss Eva's front room looked just the same as always. Miss Eva's bedroom looked just the same as it always did . . .

. . . but today Miss Eva held Adam Sumner's red balloon tight in her hand and something mysterious . . .

. . . and magical happened!

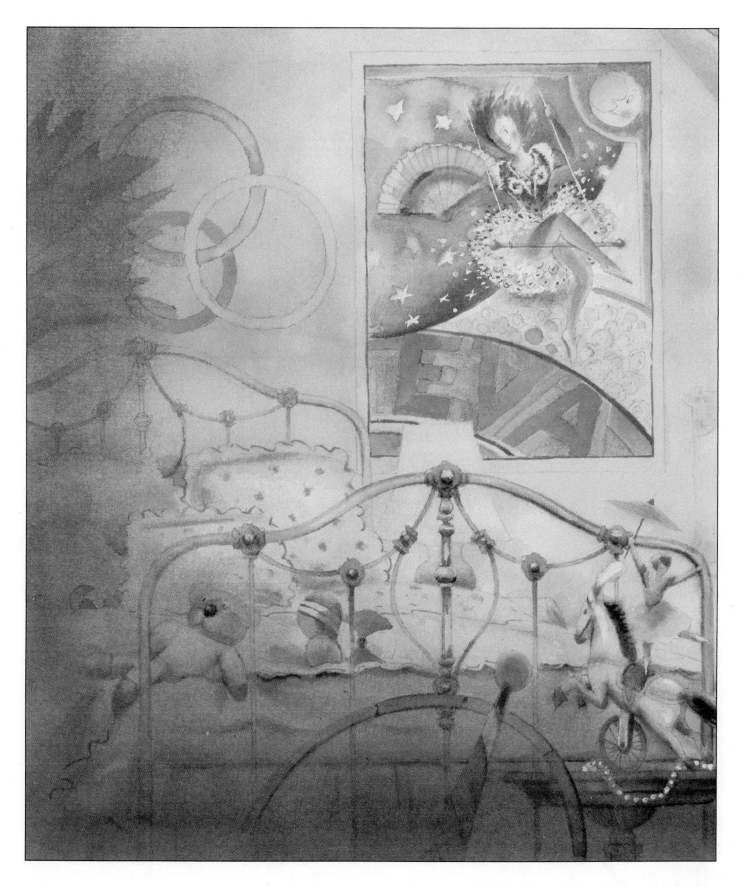

The poster in Miss Eva's room began to grow . . .

and grow. The circus came to life!

Soon music began to play, and the lights from the mirrored ball spun off like stars and swirled into the night.

The neighbors heard the music and followed the lights to Miss Eva's window.

The circus performed its magic for Miss Eva's friends into the early hours of the morning. Best of all was Miss Eva, who flew through the night on the wings of her red hair.

The next day Miss Eva didn't wear the same black dress she wore every day. She passed Spencer's Market and waved to Mr. Spencer, just as she did every day. She walked across the street while Mike the policeman held the traffic, just as he did every day.

But today someone new holds Adam Sumner's red balloon.

THINK IT OVER

1. What was Miss Eva like before she took the balloon home? What was she like after?
2. What could you do to make someone's day special?

WRITE

What do you think will happen to Mike the policeman? Write a story about what happens when Mike takes the balloon home.

SPECIAL TIMES

Do you think Miss Eva would enjoy the fiesta? Tell why you think as you do.

· ·

Would you like to join the Cinco de Mayo celebration in Mexico, or would you rather see the circus? Explain why.

· ·

WRITER'S WORKSHOP

What if Miss Eva had given the red balloon to you? Would you have changed? If so, how? Draw a picture of yourself before you got the red balloon and after. Write a sentence under each picture to tell about it. Then share your work with your classmates.

CONNECTIONS

MUSIC DAY

Louis W. Ballard is part Cherokee Indian and part Quapaw Indian. He grew up with his grandmother and grandfather in Spring River, a Native American reservation in Oklahoma. They often went to celebrations in their neighborhood. Louis learned the songs and dances so that he could join in.

Today Louis Ballard is known for writing music. His ideas come from Native American stories and songs. His music is performed all over the world and has won many prizes.

■ Have a Music Day! Work with a group to learn a Native American song or other songs. You may want to use instruments. Perform the songs for your classmates.

270

THE FIRST PEOPLE

Indians lived in this country before any other people came here to live. Read a book about Native Americans. Write what you learn on a web. Share what you know.

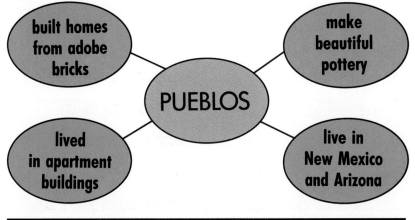

built homes from adobe bricks

make beautiful pottery

PUEBLOS

lived in apartment buildings

live in New Mexico and Arizona

SOCIAL STUDIES/MUSIC CONNECTION

LET'S SING!

Songs and chants are part of many Native American celebrations. Learn this Native American chant from Oklahoma. Choose a tone and sing it. Use instruments or clap along.

Group 1   **Group 2**   **All**

HE - OH   WAH   NO - HE   AY   YAH - WAH   NO - HE   AY   HE,   HO

arranged by Louis W. Ballard

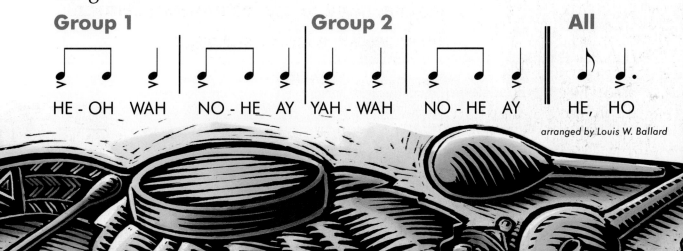

271

HANDBOOK
FOR
READERS AND WRITERS

Active Reading Strategies

A strategy is a plan for doing something. One strategy in baseball is to keep your eye on the ball. This helps you hit the ball better. Did you know there are strategies to help you read better too?

Luisa is learning how to use reading strategies. She asks herself questions before, during, and after she reads.

Before reading, Luisa uses these strategies.

✔ I **preview** the story by looking through it quickly.

✔ I think of what I know about the topic.

✔ I **predict** what the story is about. To predict means to make a good guess.

✔ I think about why I want to read this story. That's my **purpose.**

> What is the story about? Does it seem real or make-believe?

> Does anything in the story remind me of something I know or have done?

> What will happen to the characters in the story?

> What do I think I will learn?

During reading, Luisa stops and asks herself questions.

✔ I think about what I know about
  this story.

> Has anything like this ever happened to me?

✔ I think about how well
  I am reading.

> Do I understand this part? Should I read it again?

✔ I think about the words.

> Can I figure out this hard word by thinking of the meaning of the sentence?

✔ I think about my prediction.

> Is this part a surprise? Should I change my prediction?

After reading, Luisa thinks about what she has read.

✔ I think about my predictions.

> Did my predictions match what happened in the story?

✔ I think about my purpose for
  reading.

> Did I learn what I thought I would?

READING FICTION

Fiction is writing that is made up by an author. Follow Aaron as he begins to read the fiction story "Ronald Morgan Goes to Bat." The words by the story tell what Aaron does and thinks before and during his reading.

Before Aaron reads, he previews the story. He predicts what will happen from the title and the pictures.
The boy holding the bat looks worried. I know from playing baseball that he's holding the bat wrong. I think he is Ronald Morgan. It looks like he will not be able to hit the ball when it is his turn.

Aaron recalls what he already knows about playing baseball and sets a purpose for reading.
I like to play baseball a lot. I know that hitting the ball is not always easy. I want to read to see if Ronald Morgan learns how.

Ronald Morgan Goes to Bat
by Patricia Reilly Giff

Baseball started today. Mr. Spano said everyone could play.
"Even me?" I asked.
And Tom said, "You're letting Ronald Morgan play? He can't hit, he can't catch. He can't do anything."
Mr. Spano looked at me. "Everyone," he said.
"Yahoo!" I yelled. I pulled on my red and white shirt, the one that says GO TEAM GO, and ran outside to the field.

"Two things," Mr. Spano told us. "Try hard, and keep your eye on the ball."

Then it was time to practice. Michael was up first. He smacked the ball with the bat. The ball flew across the field.

"Good," said Mr. Spano.

"Great, Slugger!" I yelled. "We'll win every game."

It was my turn next. I put on the helmet and stood at home plate.

During reading, Aaron tries to picture in his mind what is happening on the ball field. *Michael can really hit the ball. This looks like a good team. But I still wonder about Ronald Morgan.*

He confirms his prediction.

My prediction was right. Ronald Morgan did not hit the ball. I still wonder if he will learn how.

"Ronald Morgan," said Rosemary. "You're holding the wrong end of the bat."

Quickly, I turned it around. I clutched it close to the end. *Whoosh* went the first ball. *Whoosh* went the second one. *Wham* went the third. It hit me in the knee.

"Are you all right?" asked Michael.

But I heard Tom say, "I knew it. Ronald Morgan's the worst."

At snack time, we told Miss Tyler about the team.

"I don't hit very well," I said.

And Rosemary said, "The ball hits him instead."

Everybody laughed, even me.

I shook my head. "I hope it doesn't happen again."

Miss Tyler gave me some raisins. "You have to hit the ball before it hits you," she said.

Aaron draws a conclusion about Ronald Morgan and makes another prediction.

Ronald Morgan is a nice person! He can laugh at what happens to him. I wonder if he'll do better the next time.

He figures out a new word.

I wonder what Miss Tyler gave Ronald Morgan. I'll try to figure it out from the sounds the letters make. Oh, it's raisins. That's right. It's snack time.

(See pages 16–27 for the story "Ronald Morgan Goes to Bat.")

READING NONFICTION

Nonfiction tells about real things. Nonfiction can be about dinosaurs, how to play checkers, or what people do on holidays. Special strategies can help you read nonfiction. One strategy is called **K-W-L**.

- **K** stands for "What I **K**now." Preview the story by reading the title and looking quickly at the pictures. Ask yourself what you already know about the topic.

- **W** stands for "What I **W**ant to Know." Think of some questions you want to answer as you read.

- **L** stands for "What I **L**earned." After you have finished reading, think about your questions. Did you get answers? Did you learn what you wanted to? Did you learn anything else?

Kareem makes a **K-W-L** chart before he reads the nonfiction story "Fiesta!" First, he follows the **K** and **W** steps and writes his ideas and questions on the chart. Then, Kareem thinks about the **W** questions as he reads.

K—What I **K**now	**W**—What I **W**ant to Know	**L**—What I **L**earned
The people are having fun. People have picnics. Children play games. There are fireworks to watch.	What is a fiesta? What is Cinco de Mayo? Who are these people? Why are they wearing those hats and clothes?	

Fiesta!
by June Behrens

We hear music, music everywhere. We sing and dance and eat and play. The fiesta in our park is like a big party. Welcome to the fiesta!

Many people wear bright and beautiful Mexican costumes. Look at the sombreros Joe and his friends are wearing. A sombrero is a hat with a very broad brim. It is almost as big as little Joe.

This is a Cinco de Mayo fiesta party. Cinco de Mayo means fifth of May. The fifth of May is a joyous festival day, a very special day for Mexican Americans. It is an important day for all the people in America.

On May 5, 1862, there was a big battle in the town of Puebla, Mexico. In a battle with the French army, the poor, ragged Mexican army won a great victory.

The victory helped to drive foreigners out of North America. No foreign power has invaded North America since. Each year, on the fifth of May, people celebrate the victory of Cinco de Mayo.

Now I understand. Cinco de Mayo is a Mexican holiday. The people celebrate this holiday to remember how the Mexican army won a victory long ago.

After Kareem read the story, he thought about what he had learned. Then he wrote what he had learned in the **L** part of his chart. What do you think he wrote?

(See pages 246–256 for the story "Fiesta!")

VOCABULARY STRATEGIES

When you read, you will find some words you don't know. What can you do when this happens? First, try skipping that word and reading more of the story. Many times you can understand the story without knowing the word. If you do need to know what a word means, these strategies can help you.

- Look at all the letters in the word. What sounds do the letters stand for? Put together all the sounds in the word. Does it sound like a word you know?

- Read the words and sentences around the word you do not know. Think about what they mean. They can help you figure out what the word that you do not know means.

- See if you know any parts of the word. For example, playground is made up of play and ground. If you know the parts, you can figure out the word.

- If these strategies don't help, use a **dictionary** or a **glossary** to find the meaning. You might also ask a classmate or your teacher for help.

When you think you have figured out what a word is, always ask yourself if it makes sense in the sentence.

Ramon is reading this paragraph about the Chinese New Year. See how he figures out new words.

This word begins like <u>fan</u>, but that doesn't help me. From the other words, though, I think <u>festival</u> means the same as <u>holiday</u>.

I can't figure out this word! Maybe if I keep reading, I'll get an idea of what it means.

Here's a long one. The first part is <u>fire</u> and the second is <u>works</u>. Oh, <u>fireworks</u>! We have fireworks on the Fourth of July.

This word tells about the time of year. The first part is <u>joy</u>. I know that means "happy." The last part is <u>-ful</u>. That means "full of." So <u>joyful</u> means "full of joy." That makes sense because a holiday is a time full of joy.

What sounds do the letters stand for in this word? It begins like <u>hat</u>. Oh, <u>holiday</u>! That makes sense because this is about New Year's Day.

Chinese people begin their New Year's <u>holiday</u> on the night of the first full moon of the year. This <u>festival</u> comes in January or February. For fifteen days the people <u>celebrate</u>. They take part in a parade with a huge paper and silk dragon. They decorate their houses and watch <u>fireworks</u>. It is a <u>joyful</u> time of year.

Now I know that <u>celebrate</u> must mean something like "to have a party."

SPEAKING

Do you feel shy when you talk to a group? Many people feel that way! These strategies can help you feel better when you speak.

- **Plan** what you want to say. When you talk to a group, think before you speak.
- **Practice** by telling a partner what you are going to say. Ask your partner to tell you how to say it better.

After reading "Ronald Morgan Goes to Bat," Chen and Tanya each wrote a story about Ronald Morgan. They read their stories to each other. As Tanya finished her story, Chen thought of a way to make the ending more exciting. Then he told Tanya that she might want to add that Ronald Morgan hits a home run.

The teacher asked the class to give talks about favorite books they had read. Sometimes Antonio feels shy and speaks too quietly in front of his classmates. So he practiced saying his book talk to Matt. Matt told Antonio to speak louder.

When Antonio told the group about his book, he spoke loudly and clearly. Everyone heard him!

LISTENING

Has anyone ever asked you to pay attention? When you **pay attention** to a speaker, you are using a strategy. Here are more strategies to help you be a better listener.

- **Have a purpose** for listening. You can listen to get directions, to learn information, or just for fun.
- **Be quiet** so you don't miss anything.
- **Respond** to the speaker in the right way. Laugh when someone gives a funny talk, but not when it is a serious one. Clap at the end to show you liked it.

Tanya listened carefully to Chen to find out how to make her story better. She thought about what he said. She liked his idea! So she decided to add Chen's idea about the home run to her story.

Antonio's classmates listened quietly to his book talk. They listened to find out if they might like to read Antonio's book. They laughed at the funny parts of the story. Then some classmates asked Antonio questions. They wanted to find out more about the story before they decided if they liked it.

THE WRITING PROCESS

There are certain steps you can follow to make your writing better. These steps are called the **writing process.** The writing process can help you write a letter to your aunt, tell a friend how to make a kite, or describe your snake to your classmates.

You should follow the steps of the writing process in order. If you don't like what you have done in any step, you can always do the step again or start over.

PREWRITING

Prewriting is the first step. Now is the time to decide what to write about and to put your ideas in order. First, ask yourself **who, what,** and **why.**

1. **Who** will read my writing? Will it be my grandfather? Will it be my best friend?
2. **What** kind of writing am I going to do? Will I write a friendly letter? Will I write a story?
3. **Why** am I writing? Is my purpose to tell how to do something? Is it to share something funny?

Next, use your imagination to think of writing ideas, or **topics.** You can also talk to your classmates to get ideas. Then, choose a topic that you and your readers will like.

Eriko asks herself **who, what,** and **why** questions.

1. Who? my cousin Masumi
2. What? a friendly letter
3. Why? to tell her something interesting

Then Eriko talks with a group about topics. Should she tell Masumi about seeing penguins at the zoo, or about catching a fly ball, or about visiting the fire station? Eriko knows that Masumi loves baseball, so she decides to write about catching a fly ball in her last baseball game.

After you have chosen a topic, put your ideas in order. You might want to make a list, a picture, or a chart to help you.

Eriko makes a flow chart to show the order in which things happened. She pictures the game in her mind. Then she draws the pictures.

DRAFTING

During **drafting,** you use the information on your list, picture, or chart to make a first try at writing. A first try is called a **first draft.**

- Write quickly. Write down as many ideas as you can.
- Do not worry about mistakes. You can make changes later.

Eriko uses her chart to help her write a first draft.

April 20, 1993

Dear Masumi,

Last Saterday I caut a fly ball in our baseball gam. i was playing second base Angela was batting. she hit the ball over my hed. It was coming down. I held my arms up. I triped and sat down. The ball fell into my glove. It did not touch the ground.

Your favorite cousin,

Eriko

RESPONDING AND REVISING

In this step, you talk about your writing with your classmates. They may have ideas for making your writing better. Then, make changes until you are happy with your work.

Eriko reads her first draft to her writing partner, Angela. Angela has some ideas.

What can I do to make my letter better?

Maybe I should write that the ball went up high.

Put the part about catching the ball at the end. Then it will be a surprise.

Yes, and tell what the coach calls you now.

Eriko makes the changes she and Angela talked about. She uses editor's marks to show the changes.

Last Saterday I caut a fly ball in our baseball
gam i was playing second base Angela was batting.
she hit the ball over my hed. It was coming down.
high
I held my arms up. I triped and sat down. The
ball fell into my glove. It did not touch the ground.
Now my coach calls me Fly Catcher

EDITOR'S MARKS	
∧	Add something.
⤶	Take out something.
⌃	Change something.
↺	Move something.

PROOFREADING

In this step you read your writing again. Check that you used capital letters and end marks correctly. Check your spelling.

When Eriko has made the changes she likes, she reads her letter again to check it for mistakes. She uses more editor's marks.

EDITOR'S MARKS	
≡ Use a capital letter.	⌒ Take out something.
⊙ Add a period.	⌃ Change something.
⌃ Add something.	⌒ Check the spelling.

Eriko should have made the word I a capital letter. She uses this mark ≡.

Eriko needs a period at the end of the sentence. She uses this mark ⊙ .

Eriko circles words that are not spelled right. She finds out how to spell them.

Last (Saterday) in our baseball (gam) i was playing
Saturday   *game*
second base⊙ Angela was batting. she hit the ball
high over my (hed). It was coming down. I held my
head
arms up. I (triped) and sat down. The ball fell into
tripped
my glove. It did not touch the ground. I (caut) a
caught
fly ball! Now my coach calls me Fly Catcher.

Eriko should have started the sentence with a capital letter. She uses this mark ≡ .

Eriko checks her spelling carefully. Here are some things she looks for.

- She looks for words that should have double letters. She adds a <u>p</u> to <u>triped</u> to make <u>tripped</u>.

- She looks for words that have silent letters. She puts the silent <u>e</u> in <u>game</u>.

- She checks words that have two vowels together. She makes sure she has put in all the vowels. She adds an <u>a</u> to <u>hed</u> to make <u>head</u>.

When Eriko can't figure out how to spell a word, she looks it up in the dictionary or the glossary or asks someone how to spell it.

PUBLISHING

In the **publishing** step, you share your writing. First, make a neat copy. Then, think of an interesting way to share it with others.

Eriko makes a neat copy of her letter in her best handwriting. She is careful to fix all the mistakes. A good way for Eriko to share the letter is to send it to Masumi. She puts it in an envelope and writes the addresses clearly. She remembers to put a stamp on the envelope.

Before Eriko mails the letter to Masumi, she glues the letter to a piece of cardboard and cuts it into big puzzle pieces. Masumi will have fun putting the puzzle together so she can read the letter.

THE LIBRARY

If someone asked you what a library is, what would you say? Is it a building or room full of books? Is it a place to read stories? Is it somewhere to find out information? All three things are true about a library.

A library has two kinds of books—**fiction books** and **nonfiction books.** Fiction books are stories made up by authors. Some stories seem very real, and some are make-believe.

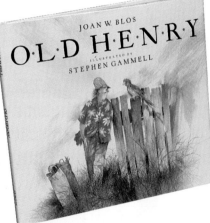

This fiction book is a story about a man who moves to a new neighborhood. It is made up, but it seems real.

Nonfiction books are about real people, places, and things. You can use them to find information.

Here is a nonfiction book that tells why May fifth is a holiday to the Mexican people.

296

Fiction books are kept together in one place in the library. They are put on the shelves in ABC order by their authors' last names. Nonfiction books are kept in another part of the library. They are in groups by their subjects. All the nonfiction books about fish would be together.

Most libraries have a computer or a **card catalog** to help you find books. The card catalog has cards for every book in the library. The cards are in ABC order by the first word on the card. You can find a book by looking for a card with its title or with the author's last name.

title card

E	**Little Penguin's Tale**
	Little Penguin's Tale / written and illustrated by Audrey Wood.
	Harcourt Brace Jovanovich
	c1989

Look under **L**.

author card

E	Wood, Audrey
	Little Penguin's Tale / written and illustrated by Audrey Wood.
	Harcourt Brace Jovanovich
	c1989

Look under **W**.

TEST-TAKING STRATEGIES

You can use strategies when you take tests. There are things you can do **before**, **during**, and **after** a test. They will help you do your best.

Before the test, you should study.

- Remember what you and your class read and talked about.
- You might talk to a partner about what you have learned.
- Read information again that might help you on the test.
- Think about what you have learned.

During the test, do these things.

- Listen carefully to what the teacher says.
- Read all the directions before you start.
- Do the easy questions first. Then go back and work on the harder ones.

Use these special strategies to help yourself answer different kinds of questions. One kind of test question asks you to choose an ending for a sentence. Look at this one.

1. Ronald Morgan has trouble hitting the baseball because

   ◯ the bat is too heavy.

   ◯ he closes his eyes.

   ◯ his friends talk to him.

- Read the sentence and all the answers.
- Think about the story.
- Decide which answer matches the story.
- The answer <u>he closes his eyes</u> is correct. On a test like this you would shade in the bubble.

● he closes his eyes.

Another kind of question asks you to choose a word from a box to finish a sentence.

dances	sombreros	costumes
parties	music	victory

1. At the Cinco de Mayo fiesta, people wear large hats called _____.

- Read all the words in the box. Then read the sentence.
- Read the sentence again, and try each word in the blank. Decide which one makes sense and matches what you read in "Fiesta!"
- On a test you would write <u>sombreros</u> on the line.

After you finish the test, use these strategies.

- Read the questions and your answers. Check your work.
- Make sure you have written or marked your answers clearly so the teacher can read them.
- Make sure you have answered each item.

GLOSSARY

The **Glossary** can help you understand what words mean. It gives the meaning of a word as it is used in the story. It also has an example sentence to show how to use the word in a sentence.

The words in the **Glossary** are in ABC order. ABC order is also called **alphabetical order.** To find a word, you must remember the order of the letters of the alphabet.

Suppose you wanted to find *gigantic* in the **Glossary.** First, you find the **G** words. **G** comes near the middle of the alphabet, so the **G** words must be near the middle of the **Glossary.** Then, you use the guide words at the top of the page to help you find the entry word *gigantic.* It is on page 304.

A **synonym,** or word that has the same meaning, sometimes comes after an example sentence. It is shown as *syn.*

meaning

entry word—[**gi·gan·tic**   Very big: **The *gigantic* dinosaur is too big to fit under the bridge!** *syn.* huge

example sentence

synonym

picture —

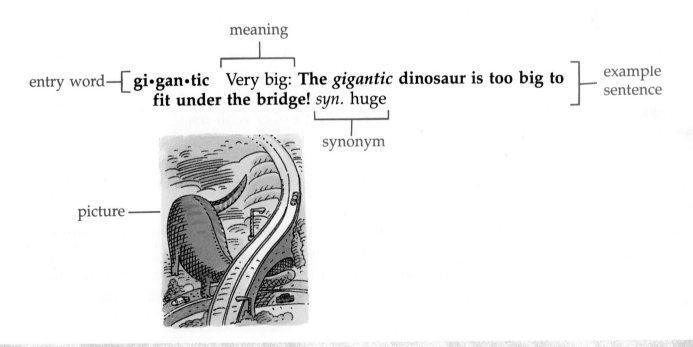

awake

A

a·fraid   Scared: **Some people are** *afraid* **of the sound of thunder.** *syn.* frightened

al·lowed   Let someone do something: **You are** *allowed* **to ride my bike.**

al·read·y   Before a certain time: **The boys were** *already* **in the circus tent when the clowns ran in.**

an·swered   Picked up a telephone when it rang and began to speak; opened the door when the doorbell rang: **Jenny** *answered* **the phone and said "hello" to her dad.**

a·wake   Not asleep: **My cat stays** *awake* **all night and sleeps all day.**

B

be·gan   Started: **Ana's day** *began* **when her alarm clock rang.**

both·ered   Made upset or angry: **We were** *bothered* **by bugs crawling on our legs as we sat in the tall grass.**

brought   Took along: **Eric** *brought* **nuts to the park for the squirrels.**

bus·y   Having a lot to do; working: **Carlos was** *busy* **at home and couldn't play with us.**

celebrate

C

care   To look after or to keep watch over: **Grown-ups take** *care* **of children.**

cel·e·brate   To do certain things during a special time: **We** *celebrate* **the Fourth of July by watching fireworks.**

closed Shut: **Mrs. Rivera** *closed* **the window so that no rain would come in.**

cried Yelled or shouted: **"Look out!" Lori** *cried* **as the pile of books began to tip.**

closed

D

de·cid·ed Made up one's mind: **I** *decided* **to paint the fence brown instead of blue.**

de·li·cious Very good to eat: **A peach is a sweet,** *delicious* **fruit.** *syn.* tasty

dif·fer·ent Not the same as the rest: **This yellow leaf is** *different* **from the green ones.**

dis·cov·ered Found: **Victor** *discovered* **a beautiful shell in the sand.**

dis·grace Something to feel ashamed of; a mess: **The playground is a** *disgrace* **with the trash and papers all over it.**

discovered

E

ear·ly Near the beginning of a time; not late: **We went to the movie** *early* **so that we could buy popcorn before it started.**

earned Got something by doing work: **Our class** *earned* **a prize because we picked up the most trash from the playground.**

edg·es The lines or places where an object ends: **The** *edges* **of the table feel sharp.**

e·ven Besides that; also: **Carrots taste sweet and are** *even* **good for you.**

ex·cept But not: **All the flowers grew,** *except* **the one that did not get water.**

edges

field

floor

gigantic

F

fair Giving everyone the same chance: **Mr. Osato is** *fair* **because he lets everyone have a turn feeding the fish.**

fa·vor·ite A person or thing that is liked the best: **I asked for strawberry because it is my** *favorite* **kind of ice cream.**

feel·ings The part of a person that can be happy or sad: **You hurt my** *feelings* **when you don't smile at me.**

fes·ti·val A big party that takes place on a holiday or at another special time: **We were singing, dancing, and eating at the spring** *festival.*

field A piece of land used for sports: **We went out to the** *field* **to play baseball.**

fi·nal·ly At last; at the end: **After traveling for two days, we** *finally* **got to Grandma's house.**

fin·ished Done: **Mr. Chen put the paints away after his painting was** *finished.*

floor A level of a building: **Rosa lives on the top** *floor* **of the tall building.**

for·get To have something go from your mind; the opposite of *to remember:* **I** *forget* **my dreams as soon as I wake up.**

fright·ened Scared: **The dogs barked and** *frightened* **the birds away.**

G

gath·ered Came together into one place: **My friends and I** *gathered* **at the big tree to play ball.**

gi·gan·tic Very big: **The** *gigantic* **dinosaur is too big to fit under the bridge!** *syn.* huge

hap·pi·ly In a happy way: **The baby played** *happily* **with his toys.** *syn.* joyfully

heard Took in sounds through the ears: **We** *heard* **dogs barking in the park.**

hur·ried Moved quickly: **Jason** *hurried* **into the house when it started to rain.**

heard

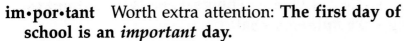

im·por·tant Worth extra attention: **The first day of school is an** *important* **day.**

in·vit·ed Asked someone in a nice way to do something: **Gena** *invited* **all her friends to come to her birthday party.**

joined Got together with someone: **Angela jumped into the water and** *joined* **the other swimmers.**

listens

learned Found out how to do something: **Tyrone** *learned* **to sing every word in the song.**

lis·tens Pays attention to a sound: **Juan** *listens* **to hear what his mother whispers to him.**

moves   Goes to live in a new place: **The family** *moves* **into a new house every ten years.**

noise

nev·er   Not ever: **Maya is very quiet and** *never* **yells at anyone.**

noise   A loud sound: **Did you hear the loud** *noise* **the box of dishes made when it fell?**

noth·ing   Not anything: **The goats are hungry because they have** *nothing* **to eat.**

phone

o·pened   Uncovered: **When Tami** *opened* **her eyes, she saw a big gift!**

per·fect   Best; having nothing wrong: **These fresh apples are** *perfect* **for a homemade pie.**

phone   Telephone: **I talked on the** *phone* **to my friend who lives in the next town.**

pile   A number of things set on top of each other: **Dad uses rocks from the** *pile* **to build a wall.**

plans   Ideas about what to do or how to do something: **We made** *plans* **to hike and swim at the park.**

pile

prac·tice   To do something many times to help yourself become better: **I need to** *practice* **my handwriting to make it neater.**

prey   Any animal that another animal wants to eat: **Will the mouse be the hungry cat's** *prey***?**

prob·lem   Something that is hard to answer or to know what to do about: **Mai's** *problem* **is that she wants to write, but she doesn't have any paper.** *syn.* trouble

quick

quick   Very fast: **The** *quick* **little fish swam away from the big fish.**

qui·et   Not loud or noisy: **I can go to sleep faster when it is** *quiet* **in my house.** *syn.* silent

repair

re·mem·ber   To think about something again: **I** *remember* **when I was five years old and rode a bike for the first time.**

re·pair   To fix: **Lin will** *repair* **the broken cup with glue.** *syn.* mend

round   Shaped like a circle or a ball: **A beach ball is** *round.*

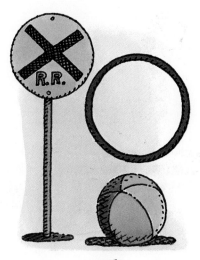

search   To try to find something: **Roberto and I will** *search* **for my lost dime in the grass.**

se·cret   Something a person knows or has and does not want anyone to know about: **I can't show you what is in my pocket because it is a** *secret.*

round

shared

shared Gave out something so that each person got a part: **The children** *shared* **the pie by each taking the same size piece.**

spe·cial Extra nice; different from the others: **Pam wears her** *special* **dress on holidays.**

stay To live somewhere for a while; to not move or go away: **We will** *stay* **at the beach house all summer.** *syn.* remain

stew A thick soup: **We ate warm** *stew* **made with meat, potatoes, and carrots for lunch.**

T

taught Helped someone learn something: **The dentist** *taught* **us how to brush our teeth the right way.**

ter·ri·ble Very big; great: **Anita had a** *terrible* **need for a drink of water after running the race.**

through

through In one side and out the other: **The train went** *through* **the tunnel.**

tired Bored with something; not interested anymore: **When I am** *tired* **of TV, I like to read a book.**

tossed Threw: **David** *tossed* **the bread crumbs to the birds.**

touch·ing Feeling something by using a part of the body: **My hand felt cold when I was** *touching* **the ice cube.**

to·ward In the direction of something; near: **We could see the puppy's cute face as he ran** *toward* **us.**

touching

tried Wanted to do something and started to do it: **Jimmy flapped his arms and** *tried* **to fly like a bird.**

turn A time for one person to do something: **Nina will have her** *turn* **to show her picture to the class after Miguel shows his.**

un·der·stands   Knows what something means: **Keno** *understands* **that dark clouds mean rain is coming.**

voice   The sound that comes out of the mouth when a person talks or sings: **We hear Kim's** *voice* **from far away when she yells.**

work

work   To do a job: **I** *work* **hard to keep my room clean.**

Acknowledgments continued

G. P. Putnam's Sons: Illustrations from pp. 15 and 26 in *Tomie dePaola's Book of Poems.* Illustrations copyright © 1988 by Tomie dePaola. Illustrations from pp. 112–113 in *Tomie dePaola's Favorite Nursery Tales* by Tomie dePaola. Illustrations copyright © 1986 by Tomie dePaola. *The Wolf's Chicken Stew,* written and illustrated by Keiko Kasza. Copyright © 1987 by Keiko Kasza.

Scholastic Inc.: Cover illustration from *Nathan's Fishing Trip* by Lulu Delacre. Copyright © 1988 by Lulu Delacre.

Simon & Schuster Books for Young Readers, a division of Simon & Schuster, Inc.: Miss Eva and the Red Balloon by Karen Glennon, illustrated by Hans Poppel. Text copyright © 1990 by Karen Glennon; illustrations copyright © 1990 by Hans Poppel.

Viking Penguin, a division of Penguin Books USA Inc.: I Love Saturday by Patricia Reilly Giff, illustrated by Frank Remkiewicz. Text copyright © 1989 by Patricia Reilly Giff; illustrations copyright © 1988 by Frank Remkiewicz. *Ronald Morgan Goes to Bat* by Patricia Reilly Giff, illustrated by Susanna Natti. Text copyright © 1988 by Patricia Reilly Giff; illustrations copyright © 1988 by Susanna Natti.

Handwriting models in this program have been used with permission of the publisher, Zaner-Bloser, Inc.

Photograph Credits

KEY: (t) top, (b) bottom, (l) left, (r) right, (c) center.

11, HBJ/Maria Paraskevas; 12–13 (all), HBJ Photo; 16, HBJ Photo; 28, Tornberg Associates; 28–29 (background), HBJ File; 30, HBJ Photo; 44, HBJ/Debi Harbin; 46, HBJ Photo; 64, 65, 67, Courtesy, Marc Brown; 70–71, HBJ/Maria Paraskevas; 86, SuperStock; 88 (both), NASA; 91 (t), HBJ/Maria Paraskevas; 91 (b), HBJ/Maria Paraskevas; 92–93 (all), HBJ Photo; 96, HBJ Photo; 107, HBJ/John Starkey/Black Star; 126, HBJ Photo; 128–129, HBJ/Maria Paraskevas; 130, HBJ Photo; 150, HBJ/Maria Paraskevas; 152, HBJ Photo; 166, Courtesy, Juanita Havill; 170, HBJ Photo; 182, Richard Sullivan/Shooting Star; 185 (t), HBJ/Britt Runion; 185 (b), HBJ/Britt Runion; 186–187 (all), HBJ Photo; 188–189, HBJ/Britt Runion; 202, HBJ Photo; 238, Madeleine Ellis; 240–242 (all), Mike Radencich/Raden Studio; 244, HBJ/Britt Runion; 246, HBJ Photo; 247–256 (all), Scott Taylor; 270, Larry Falk; 271, Allen Russell/ProFiles West; 274, HBJ/Britt Runion; 275, HBJ/Britt Runion; 277, HBJ/Les Stone; 281, HBJ/Debi Harbin; 282, HBJ/Debi Harbin; 286, 286–287, 287, HBJ/Maria Paraskevas; 288, 289, 291, 292, HBJ/Britt Runion; 294, HBJ/Les Stone; 295, HBJ/Maria Paraskevas; 296, HBJ/Earl Kogler.

Illustration Credits

KEY: (t) top, (b) bottom, (l) left, (r) right, (c) center.

Table of Contents Art

Tina Holdcroft, 4–5 (c), 8 (bl); Burton Morris, 4 (tl), 6 (tl), 7 (r), 8–9 (c); Tim Raglin, 6 (bl), 8 (tl); Peggy Tagel, 5 (tr) (br), 6–7 (c), 9 (r).

Unit Opening Patterns

Dan Thoner

Bookshelf Art

Seymour Chwast, 12–13, 92–93; Nathan Jarvis, 186–187.

Theme Opening Art

Randy Chewning, 14–15, 244–245; Karel Havlicek, 220–221; Cecelia Laureys, 188–189; Andy San Diego, 44–45; Rhonda Voo, 94–95.

Theme Closing Art

Randy Chewning, 43, 127, 269; Benton Mahan, 87, 219; Mary Thelan, 149, 243.

Connections Art

Jennifer Hewitson, 270–271; Peter Horjus, 88–89; Nathan Jarvis, 96–97, 182–183.

Selection Art

Susanna Natti, 16–27; Felicia Bond, 30–41; Marc Brown, 46–68; Richard Jesse Watson, 72–85; Keiko Kasza, 96–106; Eve Rice, 108–111; Frank Remkiewicz, 112–125; Jose Aruego & Ariane Dewey, 130–145; Christoph Blumrich, 146–148; Anne Sibley O'Brien, 152–165; Jack Graham, 168–169; Helme Heine, 170–179; Tomie dePaola, 180; Eric Hanson, 190–200; Robert Chronister, 201; Stephen Gammell, 202–218; Audrey Wood, 222–239; Mike Radencich, 240–242; Tomie dePaola, 257; Hans Poppel, 258–268.